Digital Libraries

**Digital Libraries and Collections Set**

coordinated by
Fabrice Papy

# Digital Libraries

*Interoperability and Uses*

Fabrice Papy

ELSEVIER

First published 2016 in Great Britain and the United States by ISTE Press Ltd and Elsevier Ltd

ISTE Press Ltd
27-37 St George's Road
London SW19 4EU
UK

www.iste.co.uk

Elsevier Ltd
The Boulevard, Langford Lane
Kidlington, Oxford, OX5 1GB
UK

www.elsevier.com

For information on all our publications visit our website at http://store.elsevier.com/

British Library Cataloguing-in-Publication Data
A CIP record for this book is available from the British Library
Library of Congress Cataloging in Publication Data
A catalog record for this book is available from the Library of Congress
ISBN 978-1-78548-045-4

Printed and bound in the UK and US

# Contents

# Information Retrieval, Web and Interoperability

## 1.1. Information retrieval: from theory to practice

Widespread access to the Internet and its most commonly used services, such as electronic mail, Web and, most recently, digital social networks, has led to a trivialization of information retrieval (IR) practices [GRI 11, DIN 14, DIN 07, CIA 05, ASS 02], which were in the recent past reserved for information specialists (journalists, information officers, guards, archivists, librarians, etc.) [CAT 01, DUF 01, LEF 00]. Having been introduced to the general public by the free access general search engines, IR was for several years delegated to a group of Internet surfers at the mercy of these automated indexing and retrieval systems with basic mechanisms[1], which can precisely and rapidly list a large part of the visible document production in the Web of documents [LEW 08, CHI 07, RIE 06, LEL 99].

A survey conducted in 2008[2] among 2,218 PhD students in Bretagne on their training needs in mastering scientific information revealed that 96% of

---

1 "In Google, the web crawling is done by several distributed crawlers. There is a URL server that sends lists of URLs to be fetched to the crawlers (...) The storeserver then compresses and stores the webpages into a repository. Every webpage has an associated ID number (...) The indexing function is performed by the indexer and the sorter. The indexer performs a number of functions. It reads the repository, uncompresses the documents, and parses them. Each document is converted into a set of word occurrences called hits. The hits record the word, position in document, an approximation of font size, and capitalization" [PAG 98].
2 By the URFIST (Regional Unit for Training in Scientific and Technical Information) in Rennes and the Joint Documentation Service of the University of Western Brittany.

the respondents used search engines[3] (73% very often and 23% regularly) as resources, while 53% used specialist portals, which came in second position.

Due to their algorithmic simplicity, sustained by easily modulable software architectures (*clustering* and *cloud computing*), these search tools were able to adapt to document format versatility and absorb the exponential increase in queries[4]. This technological performance has for a long time contributed to search engines being perceived as state-of-the-art retrieval systems. From a simplified IR perspective, the situation may have stayed the same, had it not been for the social turning point (Web 2.0) that took hold of the Web, and thus disrupted the spectacular technological progression in the accessibility of digital documents, by reintroducing variations in the information and digital practices.

While the conceptual approach of IR [DEN 03, MAN 02, LEF 00] is based on a systematic and methodical model that is easy to understand (Figure 1.1), when put into practice it takes multiple forms depending on the primary or secondary resources used, and above all on the technical means required (indexing and classification languages, query languages, technical tools, etc.) [TAS 14, ZOU 13, PIR 10, REP 11]. Within a short time, the multiple technological vectors in the field of document retrieval applied to natively digital information have generated a novel complexity that required employment of retrieval strategies based on precise knowledge of the technical functioning of IR systems, irrespective of their nature: "It is already true that technological devices propose retrieval solutions that the average person ignores. Surprisingly, it is often a convergence of such solutions that should be used for qualitative information" [MOE 98, p. 67].

Through the democratization of constantly evolving content production (articles, blog posts and comments) enriched with multimedia data

---

3 "What resources do you use when you search for information?" Possible answers were: laboratory documentation, library catalog, SUDOC catalog, databases, search engines, specialist portals, blogs, etc.
4 According to http://www.internetlivestats.com, 40,000 queries are sent to Google, on average, every second. In 2012, over 1,200 billion queries were sent to the world's most popular search engine (in 1998, the year when Google was established, 10,000 queries were processed daily).

[PAP 03a, PAP 99], the blogosphere[5] has disrupted the technological order established by search engine engineering. These publishing systems have facilitated content creation driven by essentially editorial logic [ANG 11, DES 09, SOU 03a], eliminating the constraints of indispensible computer skills that made it accessible to experts and specialist communication agencies that were disconnected from the publishing/online writing techniques [PAP 14b, AMG 08, TAR 07].

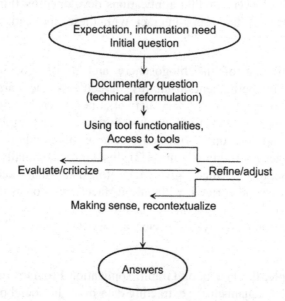

**Figure 1.1.** *The information retrieval loop (inspired by Bernard Pochet, 2008, "Knowing how to search and query" under Creative Commons License). The entry point to the figure is "the initial question" which implies a cognitive approach to information literacy, with a personal and implicit covering. In compensation, "information problem solving" aims at confronting this initial question to a first detailed explanation (without specializing it for a particular technical system) in words, terms or expressions to use (canonical or non-canonical form), excluded terms, terms to be mandatorily or optionally associated (Boolean operators). Above all, it allows the user to define the vocabulary available to describe his information expectations in various ways. It is an important stage during which the user will establish a lexical strategy for identifying generic/specific terms, either common or specialized, choice of synonyms or antonyms, etc.*

---

5 Before its dissolution and reorientation toward consulting activities, the Technorati platform consists of over 100 million blogs in 2008. Based on the data aggregated on its blog publishing platform, Wordpress.org estimates that over 50 million new posts (as well as virtual pages) and over 50 million comments are published every month. Skyrock.com, founded in 2002, counts at present 26 millions Skyblogs where 650 million published articles gather over 4 billion comments.

## 1.2. Information sources and documentary resources

During the 2000s, the worldwide frenzy of social networks [BOU 10, REB 07] and the participative and collaborative approaches have further shaken up the IR as orchestrated by the main Web search engines. "We know, for example, that Facebook is currently made up of over one million (third party) developers distributed in more than 180 countries. Facebook today consists of over 550,000 applications developed by third parties, and more than 70% of the users interact with these applications" [TCH 11, p. 60].

The functioning of the blogosphere and digital social networks is characterized by permanent instability of contents and paratextual data[6]. Blog posts, virtual pages or social networks never reach a definitive form. The object may at any time evolve during content update (insertion, modification and deletion) performed by one or more authors, depending on the assigned access rights (Figure 1.2). Instability is equally generated by social interactions, which give rise to data that accompany the primary resource and enrich it with various facets, as soon as the information is available online. Comments, evaluations, ratings, as well as readers' identity, status and quality, date, etc., are all data that lend themselves to retrieval.

For example, the Facebook Graph Application Program Interface (API)[7] is the primary mechanism for extracting data from the social platform. It is a low-level hypertext transfer protocol (HTTP) transaction-based API that can be used for data interrogation, adding data to user account, downloading all sorts of resources, etc. The Facebook data framework relies on an architecture based on nodes (things such as user, image, page, comments, etc.), edges (connections between nodes) and fields (user's date of birth, name of the page, most recent viewing date, etc.)[8]. Fields are extremely diverse and they significantly enrich nodes and edges with additional semantic data. Knowledge of these fields is, therefore, critical to reducing

---

6 Similar to footnotes, quotations or bibliographical references associated with a paragraph or phrase.
7 https://developers.facebook.com/docs/graph-api/overview/.
8 This description framework is very close to Resource Description Framework (RDF) triples, which represent type relationships (subject, predicate and object). In RDF, nodes are given by pairs (subject and object).

noise during IR (and enhancing query relevance), in particular when applied to huge sets of data[9].

Permanent instability of these objects and copresence of content data and social relations-generated data make it difficult for general search engines to index these publishing areas. On the one hand, indexing operations are performed at a pace impossible to sustain by indexing robots and on the other hand, availability of blogs and social networks would be affected by constant requests sent by robots, to the detriment of human users[10].

On top of these questions of automated indexing, there is reduced compatibility between these very generic mechanisms of blog functioning and the basic methods of search engines. Collaborative categorization, node (and connection) semantization and co-construction of fields and themes through cross-references between posts on the same site or platform (blogs being extremely simplified versions of the latter) are very badly (if at all) processed by search engine software engineering. This fact contributes to the trend of customized development in the field of IR. Due to a variety of additional scripts (plugins, add-ons and specific developments), each blog can indefinitely enrich its final information (primary data and resources) retrieval possibilities by refining them due to posts' structural data[11].

Websites, blogs and social networks thus determine contents that carry specificities translated as additional specific data that cannot be subject to similar query methods. The importance of the visibility of information systems (IS) structuring has long been known. In 1982, Y. Corson, researcher with INRIA (French national institute for computer science and applied mathematics), had already taken an interest in the psychological aspects related to database interrogation [COR 82]. He stressed the importance of the conceptual view adopted by the database organization operators, which significantly improves the IR performance when operators

---

9 Volume proportional to number of users. In 2012, Facebook stated it had over 1 billion active users.

10 "URL rewriting", a technical method for simplifying URIs that permit access to blog articles (very interesting for the users), generates false URIs that the indexing algorithms of search engines find difficult to manage, thus leading to a sort of dereferencing of the indexed pages.

11 For example, retrieval of posts whose titles contain certain terms and which contain at most three images and no videos.

have at their disposal "frameworks that reflect the types of relations existing between data".

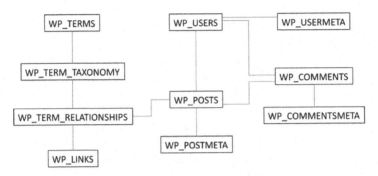

**Figure 1.2.** *Partial view of the WordPress data model (version 3.8, extracted from https://codex.wordpress.org/). The relational tables wp_term_taxonomy, wp_links and wp_term_relationships host the semantics of links and posts stored in the blog's Content Management System. The posts are connected to categories and semantic markers (tags) within the wp_terms table. The semantic links (associations) are stored in the wp_term_relationships table*

Subsequent works in cognitive psychology follow the same direction and highlight the need to have an explicit organizational structure: "Certain experiences (...) indicate that an individual modifies his IR strategies as result of own experiences and practices, as he comes to better understand the structure of the body of information, the information content and tools he has available" [DIN 02, p. 134].

These cognitive remarks are still valid today, after 20 years, in a technical documentation landscape that has significantly evolved. They plainly express the inevitable "dispersion" of IR practices within structurally different technical systems that awkwardly simulate apparent similarity by means of the input field, thus denying the different nature of disseminated resources.

## 1.3. Digital uses: IS and IR specificity

As systems for the creation, dissemination and sharing of digital contents, blogs and social platforms represent historic moments of a marked reorientation driven by digital uses. They underline an unprecedented trivialization of the production of heterogeneous contents, and furthermore, a specialization of IR practices directly related to the nature of devices the users interact with.

When applied to Web documents analyzed by the indexing robots of the search engines and lexicalized in an inverted index (term/documents vs. document/terms), IR remains relatively elementary. Advanced retrieval operations (exact phrase, Boolean operator, truncation, exclusion, language, file type, region, etc.) remain very limited and do not permit us to restrict retrieval to the structural elements of the indexed documents, as it can be done in database management systems[12] or in semantic Web-oriented systems.

These practices are now part of a set of digital competences that every citizen should have, as a prerequisite for maintaining active participation in the "information society" [UNE 05, EUR 06]. It is in this logic that for several years, driven by political initiatives, "Computer science and Internet" study programs were introduced in the curricula of schools[13] and universities, offering pupils and students the opportunity to acquire these indispensable digital competences[14].

Concurring with this need for the acquisition of new technology and information skills, a major structural evolution of the information digital universe has started [BER 08, DOU 08]. Under combined action of massive deployment of physical IS architectures and networks, governmental programs aimed at promoting the use of digital tools, economic programs

---

12 Html tags such as <head>, <title>, <meta>, <h1>, <h2>, <p>, etc., cannot be used in order to specialize a query in the search engines. It is not possible to specialize a search exclusively for documents that contain no image, necessarily making use of a <title></title> tag, of at least 3 <h2></h2> tags and for which the hits retrieval will be exclusively performed between the opening tag <h1> and the additional closing tag </h1>.

13 B2i Ecole (Diploma in Computer science and Internet) program addresses primary school pupils. It is aimed at training pupils to responsibly use digital technologies. This B2i Ecole program covers five areas. The fourth area is dedicated precisely to "inquiring, gathering information" and highlights the capacities needed to (1) read a digital document, (2) look up information in electronic media, (3) discover the abundant resources as well as the limitations of the Internet.

14 There are high stakes in the acquisition of these competences, as they are essential for free, responsible and autonomous evolution in a daily environment deeply impregnated by digital uses (C2i Portal, http://c2i.education.fr).

designed to build the actors' (whether individuals or private, public and civil organizations) confidence in the digital mutation and, finally, the establishment of poles for sustainable digital resources (citizens, schools, universities, legal, scientific, technical, etc.), numerous entirely digital information architectures were created (Gallica, service-public.fr, legifrance.fr, HAL, Universités Numériques Thématiques (Thematic Digital Universities), Canal-U, National museums, etc.). They represented a consequent evolution of dynamic Websites [SAL 99] coupling digital services to contents that are permanently organized and updated[15] [AND 12, PAP 05, ROY 03, CHA 04].

These governmental actions, designed to shape and enhance digital projects, were accompanied (sometimes preceded) by large-scale projects for the dissemination of various types of digital content, which were implemented on the market. Within several months, Youtube, DailyMotion, iTunes, Flickr, Instagram, Google Books, Facebook, etc., had become catalysts of digital contents, being sized for global coverage and elaborated according to specific organization logic.

These environments for storage and dissemination of digital content have changed their state as they reached technological and information maturity: from websites, they became portals and present themselves today as *repositories* or digital libraries. Youtube, Flickr, Wikipedia and Europeana are several examples of such documentary systems that are accessed and used on a global scale and which no longer fall under the notion of "websites" that allowed for the democratization of the Internet in the 1990s.

The repositories/digital libraries make inventories of and provide access to resources. They offer access to content made up of millions or even billions of documents, and which is constantly changing. They also organize the collaborative activity around these resources by creating and leading Internet users' communities[16], simple users or experienced

---

15 For example, service-public.fr gathers all French legal and administrative information and proposes a full range of online services: applications for civil status documents (birth, marriage or death certificates), calculation of minimal bonus for a trainee, setting an appointment with police headquarters, online fine payment, etc.

16 On Instagram, 70 million photos are shared daily by Internet users (https://instagram.com/about/us/).

developers[17]. These complex devices provide a whole variety of additional functionalities that are available upon registration, often free of charge, of a user account as a prerequisite.

Due to the complexity of technologies implemented and to the variety of user services, these systems for online dissemination of digital contents have become increasingly impenetrable – as we have seen in the case of blog platforms and social networks – to directories and general search engine indexing.

## 1.4. From websites to new technical documentation architectures

The phrase "digital library" is today widely accepted by Internet users despite the wide variety of digital documentary devices that it covers. Nevertheless, the trivialization of systems for digital information dissemination through the Web and its http/https protocols, the heterogeneity of available resources and the interoperability between contents of different technical nature have added to the growing confusion in the semantic appropriation of this phrase. The following is an extract from [SAL 05]:

> "Depending on the chosen criteria, the notion of digital library refers, in effect, to quite distinct situations; (i) When the traditional heritage notion is highlighted, then it refers to digitized documents (...); (ii) The heritage imperative also concerns digital documents, and there are huge collections online, such as the Web archives and NASA images (...); (iii) When the volume criteria is considered (for example, number of accessible pages), with the exception of the abovementioned ones, the largest collections are undoubtedly to be found in the sphere of scientific journals or academic bodies, commercial or non-commercial publishers, Elsevier and OCLC being in the first line (...); (iv) When access to books online is considered as main characteristic, then we should consider online bookstores such as Amazon, or collaborative initiatives for online access to books that are in the public domain (...). This is not an exhaustive list of criteria, and everyone could come up with lists that do not overlap".

---

17 These systems offer developers free access to Application Program Interface (API) that permits them to develop various applications for accessing and viewing data.

While attaching the "digital library" label to free access devices such as Gallica, Europeana[18], Isidore, Persee, Inatheque, Stanford Digital Repository, Wikipedia or ArXiv may seem convenient due to the nature of resources they provide access to, the same may not be readily obvious when it comes to Youtube, Vimeo, Flick, iTunes, Dailymotion, Google Books, NetFlix, Deezer, Slideshare, etc. This confusion significantly deepens as soon as the list is completed with documentary environments that do not (always) propose primary, but generally rather descriptive, data.

It is the case of WorldCat[19], the Library of Congress Catalog[20], Sudoc[21], the Virtual Library[22], the bookmarks of the National Library of France BnF[23], the contemporary music portal[24], etc., which, despite frequent inaccessibility of the primary resources, provide mechanisms inspired directly by physical libraries for the organization and description of these resources[25]. These pools of descriptive data that can be freely accessed and whose interrogation does not require particular expertise prove their high quality when resources are to be contextualized, either by the means of classifications generally used by libraries, or by means of semantic descriptors (keywords and subject authority) that allowed for homogeneous indexing. When observing a RAMEAU subject authority index card, the importance of such directories of rigorously selected[26] and regularly updated

18 Europeana Library is a project in which 27 countries of the European Union participate and consists of over 26 million digital objects: 15 million images, 10 million OCR scanned texts, 440,000 audio sequences, 170,000 videos, 7,000 3D objects, etc.
19 Proposed by OCLC Online Computer Library Center Inc., Worldcat is a bibliographical database with 2 billion references (http://www.worlcat.org).
20 http://www.loc.gov
21 http://www.sudoc.abes.fr
22 http://vlib.org
23 http://signets.bnf.fr
24 http://www.musiquecontemporaine.fr/
25 This list may be expanded to include Amazon.com, allocine.fr, khanacademy.org, etc., which offer, respectively, the possibility to look through, video extracts, fanzines, additional information on the actors, directors, shooting conditions, etc., and finally, MOOC with interactive lessons (as well as images and summaries freely provided by the libraries for a richer content).
26 By the end of December 2014, RAMEAU counted over 177,000 authority notes (out of which 107,000 are common names). RAMEAU is not a thesaurus, it is not constituted *a priori* and it is even enriched according to the indexing needs, based on proposals advanced by its users' network (300 documentary establishments and various bodies in France, Belgium and Switzerland) (according to http://rameau.bnf.fr/informations/rameauenbref.htm).

terms (Table 1.1) becomes obvious. Each term is accompanied by "facets" that allow for a better grasp of its semantic reach and the field(s) in which it is more frequently employed.

---

*Employed for:*

Green growth, eco-responsible development, durable economic development, sustainable development, viable development, eco-development, durable economy, sustainable economy and green economy

*Generic term(s):*

Economic development – environmental aspect

*Associated term(s):*

Local Agenda 21, culture and sustainable development, human development, social and solidarity economy, education for sustainable development, ecological footprint, future generations (law), sustainable development indicators, biosphere reserves, common but differentiated responsibility, sports and sustainable development, Grenelle environment (2007, Paris)

*Specific term(s):*

Sustainable agriculture, sustainable aquaculture, sustainable architecture, fair trade, sustainable consumption, sustainable building, sustainable degrowth, sustainable land development, double and triple dividends (sustainable development), ecodesign, industrial ecology, circular economy, economy of functionality, ecotourism, green jobs, green industry, sustainable lifestyle, sustainable fishing, soft technology, energy transition, sustainable transport, sustainable town planning

*LCSH equiv.:*    sustainable development

*Domain(s):*    330 / 577

---

**Table 1.1.** *Partial RAMEAU authority index card "sustainable development" (subject heading common name) (http://catalogue.bnf.fr/ark:/12148/cb12271499g/PUBLIC). The heading is accompanied by categories that aim at reducing its ambiguity. "Employed for", "Associated term", "Generic term", "Specific term" indicate the semantic positioning of the subject heading in relation to other terms. The translation into its American equivalent in the LCSH (Library of Congress Subject Heading) sets a connection with Anglo-Saxon catalogs. Domain groups can be noticed, according to Dewey Decimal Classification. Indices 330 and 577 refer, respectively, to "Political economy – general economy" and "Ecology"*

These online catalogs are not always limited to the display of metadata and they may provide access to the primary source if its digital format exists. Such is the case of PhD Theses, which are often disseminated online[27] for promotion reasons. The resource physically exists in an institutional repository (theses.fr) or in the IS (digital library) of the concerned university and is assigned a perennial Uniform Resource Identifier (URI). Irrespective of the storing location, the resource is visible and accessible due to the catalog, though this is not a server for storing associated data files.

## 1.5. Digital libraries: between library and computer science

The phrase "digital library" in itself generates permanent exchanges that do not inquire only the technological bases of documentary devices, but also their documentary relevance, usability[28] by very wide audiences, cognitive interoperability [FAV 13, FEY 07] and capacity to evolve and integrate structured environments [LET 14, ESC 10]: "A digital library does not serve only as an archive of relevant information; it should have extended prerogatives and propose a more comprehensive functional use pattern" [BER 12, p. 131].

The existence of these digital documentary artifacts is closely linked to the industrialization of digitization procedures aimed at (i) better (less expensive) management and conservation of heterogeneous documentary resources (text, image, video, sound, etc.), (ii) enhanced use (in the broad sense) of digital and digitized resources and (iii) wider access to (use of) digital resources. In other words, it is a convergence of digital technologies, documentary techniques and user cognitive processes that reveal the complexity of digital libraries in terms of use and appropriation by potential users.

The phrase "digital libraries" is a bridge between two realms of undeniable complexity: on the one hand, the library and, on the other hand, computer science and its extension into information and communications technologies (ICTs). The library is thus associated with problems and even assumed missions related to sustainability, heritage, dissemination,

---

27 Subject to the author's permission.
28 ISO 9241-1998, Part 11: Guidance to usability [ISO 98]: "Extent to which a product can be used by specified users to achieve specified goals with effectiveness, efficiency and satisfaction in a specified context of use".

organization, accessibility, sharing, conservation, use, etc. More than ever, it is a dense, rich and complex universe. According to the first UNESCO World Report [UNE 05], the library occupies a central place among the economic challenges of the new information paradigm, since the start of the digital era and the recent emergence of the "Society of Information and Knowledge" [MAT 05, MAT 01]. Finally, the adjective "digital" is a reflection of computer engineering and the wide field of ICT. These two universes, generators of significant knowledge and know-how, have evolved in relative separation until the massive deployment of ICT and the Internet tidal wave.

Today, they are closely intertwined as a result of the technical–industrial initiatives and governmental policies involved in building an "information society". These universes complement and influence one another and compete for the dominant position in matters related to the organization of documentary resources, either traditional, digital or digitized: physical libraries that have few computerized systems, fully virtualized and, interoperable libraries, and finally, hybrid libraries that, based on century-old principles of document organization, attempt to associate immaterial with material (for example, the OPAC[29]), local with distant (open/closed/semi-open client-server architecture) and visible with invisible (semantic data on the bibliographical notes).

From a technological point of view, there is no essential difference between various platforms for digital contents storage and dissemination. The slight variations between content rendering plugins (streaming)[30] do not call into question the similar evolutive software architectures that they employ, the document formats[31] or the technologies that are essentially those developed and disseminated by the World Wide Web Consortium[32].

---

29 Online Public Access Catalog
30 These plugins are software extensions integrated to most of the recent Web browsers. Flash Player and Adobe PDF Reader are the most well known. Specialized plugins such as those of Amazon or Google Books permit us to look through part of the digitized works due to textual streaming (*streaming media*).
31 The best practices guide edited by Huma-Num, the Very Large Facility (Très Grande Infrastructure de Recherche (TGIR), refers to formats, standards and practices that are today the most stable in the digital field and attempts to meet the needs of those interested in launching a digital project or scaling up existing digital corpus (http://www.huma-num.fr/sites/default/files/guide_des_bonnes_pratiques.pdf).
32 www.w3.org/standards: Web design and applications, Web of devices, Web architecture, Semantic Web, XML Technology, Web of Services, Browsers and Authoring tools.

The same is true from a conceptual point of view, as the matter is to provide digital contents, despite the media variety (text, video, audio and image), through a normalized technological channel (multimedia computer, Web, smartphone, tablets, etc.) to Internet users whose information and cognitive profiles vary widely and whose expectations and needs are difficult to evaluate.

It seems, therefore, reasonable that Internet users perceive these various types of systems that offer online digital content as "digital libraries" for which simplified retrieval mode has become a rule. When looking up videos on Youtube, searching resources in BnF catalog, articles on HAL[33] or Wikipedia, etc., we have to express an interrogation in natural language and fill in an entry form reduced to essentials, which became popular with Google's contribution.

Beyond their variations, digital libraries converge toward technical functionalities and services that Internet users would from now on expect to find. In the end, the various architectures initiated by governmental or institutional programs, commercial enterprises or economic projects tend to shape the digital landscape and become structuring elements that the users handle and integrate in their common IR practices.

In spite of the aspirations toward distinctiveness or monopoly that can be guessed beyond each of these digital libraries, sustainability is not guaranteed by the technological model, but is acquired through the uses that each environment attempts to open up and carefully conserve. The acquisition of these data is meant to help in understanding the users' needs and thus anticipating their demands in order to provide them with an original service that will keep the audience at the highest level.

## 1.6. Web interoperability

Despite the high competitiveness of this technological universe that for audience reasons seeks to reduce the Internet users' hypertextual nomadism, the usual practices of associativity and hypertext in Web browsing remain firmly embedded. Websites viewing and, to a higher degree, IR, invariably

---

33 https://hal.archives-ouvertes.fr is a hybrid digital library that gathers descriptive data from articles (1,019,543) and primary resources (351,517).

lead to perpetual reading discontinuities[34], as one environment may at any time be abandoned in favor of another[35].

The free browsing of the Web digital space guided only by the user's intuitions is, however, an irrevocable invariant: "We should keep in mind that hypertext allows first of all for the calculation and presentation capacities of a computer to be put in the service of information, either structured or not, through associations between elements of various natures, which are managed by the user's intelligence or intuition" [BAL 96, p. 18].

The first Web portals (AOL, Excite, MSN, Lycos, etc.) sought to reduce the negative effects of hypertextual browsing (cognitive and informational overload, disorientation) by gathering under the same Uniform Resource Locator (URL) a set of pieces of information from distinct sites (Figure 1.3). These portal-sites relied on a meta-search engine that regularly absorbed a subset of pages from partner sites and aggregated them under a homogeneous presentation. The pages from partner sites offered an enhanced "interoperability character" to the extent that their native HyperText Markup Language (HTML) structures were designed to facilitate re-exploitation of the information on the page in the documentary context of the portal.

The Internet Trellis architecture [SER 00, LEV 98] made possible the emergence of the Web of documents by trivializing technical communication between the documents servers (Web servers). This transparency of communications has contributed to the adoption of a cooperative documentary model instrumented by hypertext. Web interoperability thus refers to technological instruments (specifications, guides, tools and software) dedicated to the construction of a globalized network of data and documents. From the first technological achievements of Berners-Lee in 1990 (HTML, HTTP and URI)[36] to the current digital social networks, the

---

34 The integration of a search bar in the Web browser, which spares search engines from having requests placed on their home page, stresses this logic of breakdown. Browsers provide the possibility of selecting one or more words on the page which is being read and then to use them to start a search in an information retrieval system.

35 Even when Internet users identify on secure sites, they are free to type a different URL in the current navigation bar or open a new one or access a different site, should they need to access another service.

36 http://webfoundation.org/about/vision/history-of-the-web/.

concept of interoperability, in the sense of set of technological means in the service of information, is a constant presence.

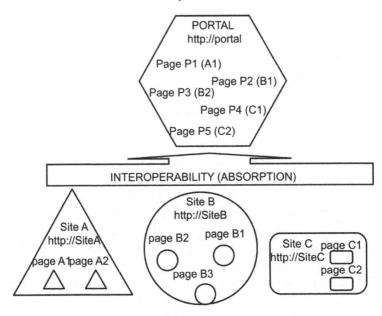

**Figure 1.3.** *Rudimentary interoperability through content aggregation/duplication. The A, B and C sites and the PORTAL portal are accessible through their URL: http://SiteA, http://SiteB, http://SiteC et http://portal. The portal, which contains its own pages, takes over either partially or entirely each site's webpages (the content of these pages may be partially or integrally taken over) which will be rendered by the portal in a way that respects the graphic standards and the viewing mechanisms*

Information technologies continue to play an important role in Web interoperability, but the founding works of Berners-Lee refer to providing users, irrespective of their technical skills, with the benefits of efficient computer equipment, bringing them up to the level required by their use. The hypertext reading, intuitive and readily available in the massively distributed documentary architecture, relies on software engineering embedded in Web browsers, high-level communication protocols between Web servers (HTTP) and lower level ones between computer servers connected to the world network (Wide Area Network (WAN), Transmission Control Protocol – Internet Protocol (TCP-IP), Domain Name Service (DNS), etc.). The continuous technological developments of the Web in a modern society that is itself technical-scientific have sometimes reversed the "technique for use" order that Berners-Lee had sought to establish. Constant innovation of equipment, applications and services has delighted the general public with technological possibilities that are in contrast with the persistence and stability of problems related to the need of information and initiatives that they generate in terms of IR [DIN 14, DEN 06, LEC 97, AR 88].

## 1.7. Interoperability for use: RSS

W3 recommendations have led to the development of a significant set of tools and software, and this has to a certain extent overshadowed the use purposes traditionally assigned to Web technologies.

Thus, the logic of interoperability as expressed in the creation of portals backed by information sites corresponds to a more subtle, still significant evolution toward availability of thematic documentary environments that are as complete as possible. Operating modes based on the absorption of pages and the transposition of their contents under other presentation models met this objective.

This elementary organization of interoperability relies on a construction in which a "beneficiary" site (the portal) gathers information extracted from "provider" Websites. This rudimentary form of technological interoperability is not symmetrical, in the sense that "provider" sites are not recipients of the data aggregated by the portal. The immediate interest of each provider site is to potentially benefit the audience and Web traffic generated by these information superstructures.

In this precursory model, the technological component relies above all on the automated software for the absorption and dynamic recomposition of distant pages that prefigure today's sophisticated interoperability modalities employed by Web services: "Interoperability is the ability for two different implementations of web services to communicate with one another. Interoperability is perhaps the most critical feature of web services, without which communication is not possible. Interoperability requirements typically exist at all layers of the protocol stack from the communication protocol and data encoding used, to higher layer application semantics such as transaction and security contexts. In the world of web technology interoperability is made possible via protocols such as HTTP, SMTP and SSL, with support from encoding formats such as MIME" [SCO 01].

In the specific case of this modern implementation expressed by G. Scott and revisited by W3, interoperability requires dedicated software mechanisms and specific data formats. Between this modern conception (which brings in notions of security and applicative semantics[37]) and the above mentioned portal version, technical sophistications have reconfigured a software conception of interoperability in which the matters of interest concern protocolized communication (security) and data exchanges between dedicated applicative systems.

Prior to Web Services (for cooperation between server applications) and AJAX[38] architecture (for client/server exchange) becoming widespread in terms of technological interoperability (development driven by the strong dominance of software engineering in the absence of which such methods are impossible to implement), another form of interoperability, employed by flows of data in Really Simple Syndication (RSS)[39] format (Table 1.2), was for a long time popular among Internet users.

In this adaptation of interoperability, technology had quite a low profile presence, assuming essentially the form of data format (tags and grammar). This may be interpreted as a sign of true cautiousness in the software mechanization will, aimed at avoiding to stifle the use prerogatives manifested by the Internet users in their already current practices of information cross-checking, aimed at customized contextualizing of a set of information extracted from the Web.

---

37 In the primitive version of interoperability presented in Figure 1.3, corresponding to an instant in the Internet evolution, the risks for the provider sites to be absorbed (today, we would say harvested) by any spider were very high and the means of protection were ineffective. Indeed, the Web agents in charge with page indexing could ignore the exclusion clauses and even escape being detected by the provider site Web server by pretending to be a simple Internet browser. A diversion of this method is at the origin of building link farms aimed at artificially increasing a site's or group of sites' popularity reflected by improved search engine ranking (spamdexing).

38 Asynchronous JavaScript and XML are a set of techniques (HTML, CSS, Javascript, XML, DOM, etc.) used in browsers to create asynchronous Web applications (for example, the input fields dynamically prefilled with self-completing object clauses propositions).

39 Rich Site Summary, RDF Site Summary and Really Simple Syndication represent, from the latest to the oldest, the semantic evolutions under RSS initials.

```
<?xml version='1.0' encoding='UTF-8'?>
<rss xmlns:rdf=http://www.w3.org/1999/02/22-rdf-syntax-ns#
        xmlns:atom="http://www.w3.org/2005/Atom"
        xmlns:taxo="http://purl.org/rss/1.0/modules/taxonomy/"
        xmlns:media="http://search.yahoo.com/mrss/"
        xmlns:dc="http://purl.org/dc/elements/1.1/"
        xmlns:itunes="http://www.itunes.com/dtds/podcast-1.0.dtd" version="2.0">
<channel>
<atom:link href="http://www.nytimes.com/services/xml/rss/nyt/Science.xml" rel="self"
type="application/rss+xml" />
<title>NYT &gt; Science</title>
<link>http://www.nytimes.com/pages/science/index.html?partner=rss&amp;emc=rss</li
nk>
<description>Science</description>
<language>en-us</language>
<copyright>Copyright 2015 The New York Times Company</copyright>
<pubDate>Thu, 23 Jul 2015 03:27:46 GMT</pubDate>
<lastBuildDate>Thu, 23 Jul 2015 03:27:46 GMT</lastBuildDate>
<ttl>2</ttl>
<image>
<title>NYT &gt; Science</title>
<url>http://graphics8.nytimes.com/images/misc/NYT_logo_rss_250x40.png</url>
<link>http://www.nytimes.com/pages/science/index.html?partner=rss&amp;emc=rss</li
nk>
</image><item><atom:link href="http://www.nytimes.com/2015/07/23/us/daily-hiv-
drug-regimen-is-effective-in-african-women-study-
says.html?partner=rss&amp;emc=rss" rel="standout" />
```

**Table 1.2.** *RSS file that gathers the day's Science dedicated articles offered by the American daily "The New York Times". Over 60 RSS flows are automatically updated by this newspaper CMS. Through various aggregation devices, these flows allow the Internet users to select and extract content from Nytimes.com. Irrespective of the information fields processed, the titles, summaries and links in these RSS flows are systematically integrated according to the RSS tag typology (<title>, <pubDate>, <language>, <url>, <link>, <image>, etc.). A full description of the latest RSS version (RSS 2.0) is available at http://cyber.law.harvard.edu/rss/rss.html*

A whole range of tools (either online, such as NetVibes, Google Reader, Planet, FreshRSS, etc., or downloadable on a computer station, such as Alterinfo[40], NewzCrawler, FeedDemon, BlogNatvigator, etc.) was developed

---

40 AlertInfo is an RSS feed reader. It is above all the initiative of GESTE, an association of content editors and online services who wanted to propose an individual technical device that met the expectations of a public acquainted with online digital content. The application consists of more than 900 pre-installed RSS threads that the user can very easily adapt and enhance.

to meet the demands of Internet users for gathering (depending on their interests) various sources of information (Figure 1.4). The density of information produced and the frequency of its updating on blogs, daily publications, e-magazines, journals, etc., explain to a great extent the reasons why Internet users have taken hold of these syndication tools. Without requiring computer science expertise, these technologically simple solutions facilitated downloading RSS documents and integrated them as subsites of the online aggregator. On the contrary, we may be surprised by the scarcity of technical functionalities available to the user[41], while the Web software editors (either free or commercial) have a tendency to consider Web browsers and participative sites as toolboxes whose functionalities need to adapt to the evolution of the users' needs. The logic of extension by means of widget, plugins, add-ons, reader, apps, etc., have meanwhile become widespread.

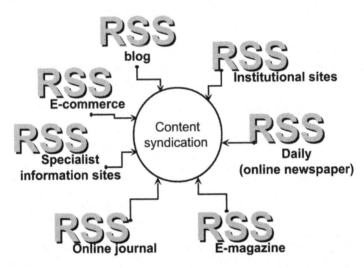

**Figure 1.4.** *Content syndication in the form of RSS feed. Interoperability consists of the functional complementarity between the device in charge with RSS feed aggregation and the sites that provide data. The functional existence of the aggregator site is directly dependent on RSS documents regularly generated by the information producing sites. This compact method permits us to gather contents of audio-visual programs of specialized sites: Web TV, YouTube channels, Web Radio, etc.*

41 For the main part of tools for feed management (subscription/unsubscription), management of filters that permit the selection of feed items and the organization of the aggregator home page.

When observed more closely, the question of aggregators lacking technical functionalities can be linked to the overinstrumentation, which, while posing its own cognitive problems, introduces a gap in the initial activity of individuals. The selection of sources of information that can be aggregated (activity related to an IR subprocess), the operations of filters on RSS feeds and the coherent organization of the aggregative object represent (Figure 1.5), finally, activities of real intrinsic complexity which lead the users to cognitive overload [CLE 07, CHE 04, CHA 02b, NOE 97, RAB 95].

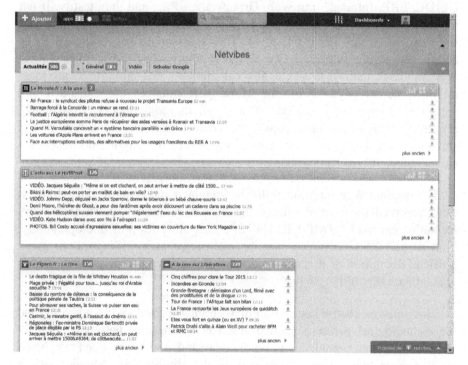

**Figure 1.5.** *RSS content aggregation in NetVibes. The very sober display pattern serves extremely precise functionalities. The themes created by the Internet user (news, general, video, etc.) appear in distinct tabs. Each tab gathers various RSS feeds. Our example focuses on the "News" tab, in which each frame presents an RSS feed (Le Monde.fr, Huffington Post, Le figaro.fr and Liberation.fr) which indicates in the title bar the number of unread feeds. For each feed, certain information associated with RSS items are displayed (here the title and the hour of publication). The update is done manually by the Internet user at any time on each feed, when its session is open. If not, Netvibes proceeds to update the feeds depending on the editor's posting frequency, popularity of the feeds and services contracted by the Internet user (chargeable services have higher priority)*

Technological interoperability, such as it was conceived in terms of articulation between documents/RSS syndication feed and the *ad hoc* compilation mechanisms, may seem rudimentary in a rapidly growing technological context, which is supposed to accompany and even anticipate the users' expectations/needs [RIE 06, CHA 01]. Conversely, it can be analyzed from the standpoint of designers who understand the stakes and the risks of technology overinstrumentation: "It should be noted that computer environments aimed at facilitating cooperation and organization of digital information have existed for many years and under various forms: GED, GEIDE, ERP, Intranet, IntraWeb, Groupware, 2P,... and they testify, if not to failure, at least to inadequacy to the situations and activities they are supposed to equip" [PAP 04, p. 6]. This assessment, psychological in its nature, is closely linked to two different approaches: "According to the 'system view', man (that we can also call subject), task and artifact are to be all three perceived as a system whose performances are expanded and enhanced compared to those of any of its components. Conversely, according to the 'personal view', the artifact changes the nature of the subject's task. This latter is thus modified and restructured and impacts the subject himself" [BOU 06, p. 33].

The original Web interoperability as imagined and conceived by Berners-Lee preserved the central role of the user in relation with an elementary technological triad HTML/URI/HTTP[42]. This other form of interoperability, built around RSS resources, may be interpreted as a willingness to avoid artificial disruption of this admittedly fragile cognitive activity of the user[43] [CHA 07a, DEN 03].

This anthropocentric conception of Web interoperability did not withstand the technological pressure exerted whereas the frontier between computer science and telecommunications, on the one hand, and Internet and telephony, on the other hand, faded away and finally disappeared. Mobile devices (laptops, smartphones, tablets, etc.), which merge electronics, computer science and telephony, propose a range of common software applications

---

42 Since studies, researches and tools, etc., referring to IR [CHI 07] date from well before the works of T. Berners-Lee, we can think that the absence of information retrieval systems in his successful scientific and technical proposition is caused by neither lack of scientific intuition nor ignorance of the instrumental demands linked to IR.

43 While it is a well known fact that "too much information kills information", too many instruments damage instrumentation.

(browser, mail, office automation, player, reader, etc.) which address the general public with little developed or undeveloped technical and information skills, have led to a reversal of priorities set by the user paradigm, for the benefit of the system paradigm.

Under the cover of accompanying novel uses related to the great digital mutation, the users were integrated into a powerful spiral of production of applications[44] whose breathtaking number is an indicator of compliance with the creed of ergonomics psychologists "design for use/design in use". Due to flexible and rapid development methods (manifesto for agile software development), software instrumentation in the name of "User Experience" (UX) got carried away and has distorted the interpretation of the technological interoperability maintained under the control of user's mature uses. The ease with which applications are produced, by means of standardized software solutions[45], for the devices used by millions of users, has called into question the IT development cycles in which the user was expected to participate, as a guarantor for quality.

This inflated production has modified the way in which users formulate their requests, this being reduced to either adoption or rejection of the proposed applications. The latter are the ones to propose themselves to the users, who are *a priori* represented by abstract models. Little does it matter that these models may be insufficient or false, after multiple trial and error tests, amplified by the number of potential users, the implicit demands for use start to take shape and they are immediately implemented in a new applicative version that is reintroduced in an $n^{th}$ development/request cycle. These cycles contribute to the artificial evolution of the "UX" by guiding the

---

44 According to the statistics portal www.statistica.com (that processes 80,000 subjects extracted from 18,000 sources), over 1.5 million applications were available on Apple App Store in June 2015 (1.5 million for Google Play Store), "it seems like, despite the ever-growing number of choices available, there's a limit to how many apps people actually use. Or, to put it differently: there's an app for every need, but there's no need for every app". [RIC 14]. In comparison with the breathtaking number of mobile applications available in recent years, WordPress CMS (established in 2013 under GPL license and used at present by 60 million online blogs) can extend its characteristics and functionalities due to 40,000 downloadable plugins that can be automatically integrated in the CMS environment (https://wordpress.org/plugins/).

45 Software Development Kit (SDK) for Android is free and IOS is not expensive (approximately 90 $ per year). They can be used by any developer to create his own mobile applications.

users' needs and simultaneously proposing solutions to compensate for their insufficient skills in handling the instruments.

In fact, this orientation that places software design upstream instead of downstream from the use, where needs should be expressed, has rendered inaudible the historical discourse on a technological interoperability under the control of use. Due to the belief in an adaptive performance of technologies on the uses, strengthened by the "UX" trend, this historical approach of interoperability is perceived as outdated. State-of-the-art technological architectures are, however, caught up by the reality of non-use situations, obviously generated by a technological model that was built upon an imaginary construct of possible uses, in total isolation from expectations and real practices:

> "The digitized corpuses are to a small extent frequented because they lack visibility on the Web and there is no communication referring to their existence. Moreover, they are competing with new players coming from outside the world of culture and research who produce digitized resources and valorize them. Finally, as they become skilled in web practices, users are more demanding in terms of services. The absence of online cultural mediation, for example, may be a problem" [CHE 12, p. 10].

## 1.8. Interoperability in digital libraries

Through the technologies they employ, digital libraries have inherited collaborative properties inherent to Web interoperability. Though they all exist under the common banner of "digital library", the various platforms with heterogeneous content and variable ends will appropriate/implement technological interoperability differently, depending on the pole – technology or use – toward which the technical documentation environment will gravitate: "What is a good digital library? As was pointed out by Fuhr *et al.*, the answer to this question depends on whom you ask. It can be considered that what differentiates a good DL from a not so good one is the quality of its services and content" [GON 04, p. 98].

It is very tempting to assign uses of support-oriented interoperability to digital libraries that have cultural, scientific or educational vocation. It would be reasonable to consider that these technical documentation architectures, funded according to public policies that promote the humanist ideas of dissemination and sharing of knowledge and information[46], were configured in such a way that digital resources could be used by large audiences according to conditions of use that only users are in the position to evaluate.

While this conception is technically feasible, most of the institutional digital libraries have opted for an interoperable functioning that has indeed led to the aggregation of resources coming from various devices but whose "tonality of use" tends to maintain the user in the technical interactivity of the technical documentation environment and constrains him to think in the use terms imagined by the designers.

In fact, technological interoperability is reduced to the "federated retrieval"[47] functionality most often proposed by the documentary portals of university and research libraries to their specialist audience. Transposing this method to the general public does not call into question the necessity to maintain the "host" device, which takes charge of the results repatriation and thus ensures the audience of a captive public. This is the case of "digital universities"[48]. This portal presents itself as unique interface with a federated search engine that interrogates the 31,000 educational resources available on the higher education thematic portals, these resources having been produced by the higher education establishments and research bodies. This centralized mechanism for interrogating multiple sources is nothing but a pale evolution of what libraries had implemented for numerous years with the Z39.50

---

46 https://www.france-universite-numerique-mooc.fr/: FUN is an MOOC platform aimed at offering wide public access to high-quality courses throughout the world. The catalog of available courses is permanently enriched and a variety of courses meeting various demands are proposed.

http://www.cnrtl.fr/: The National Center for Textual and Lexical Resources (Centre National de Ressources Textuelles et Lexicales – CNRTL), created by CNRS (National Center for Scientific Research), aims at gathering in a unique portal a maximum of computerized resources and consultation tools for the study, knowledge and dissemination of French language.

Due to a mutualization of knowledge resulted from the works of various laboratories, the CNRTL optimizes production, validation, harmonization, dissemination and sharing of resources, in terms of both computerized textual and lexical data and the tools that facilitate intelligent access to their content.

47 Using a unique search form, the federated retrieval tool of a documentary portal offers the possibility to interrogate several data sources (databases and catalogs) and capture results, possibly in unduplicated form on a unique display page.

48 http://www.france-universite-numerique.fr/.

protocol[49] in order to homogenize the results of interrogations on distant digital catalogs.

In contrast, and in a surprising manner, digital libraries such as Amazon, YouTube, DailyMotion and Vimeo, which do not adhere to any of the scientific, cultural or educational objectives of institutional platforms, propose a much more open interoperability model, which encourages novel uses that are entirely left at their users' creative discretion. It is possible to recover the thumbnail image for the works, CDs and DVDs, as well as their description (back cover for the works), free of charge from Amazon.com. This functionality is widely used by online catalogs of libraries/media libraries that enrich their bibliographical notes data. In the same way, an audio-video enrichment can be made very simply starting from YouTube, DailyMotion or Vimeo platforms that produce *ad hoc* HTML technical sequence[50] to be able to integrate the link to a particular video in a webpage, blog post, RSS feed item, etc. These HTML sequences, which are not subject to any preliminary creation of user account, are expressed in their most elementary form. This gives users freedom to reuse them at their convenience in other environments that simply have in common one of the technological components of Berners-Lee's interoperability triad (HTML/URI/HTTP).

As retrieval approaches are extremely diverse, original initiatives and personal strategies may lead to unhope for results. Only by respecting (unpredictable) uses can interoperability give free course to practical organization modalities that make sense for the initiator depending on his objectives: "If reliable knowledge is what we want, then we need to connect, contextualize, globalize our information and knowledge" [MOR 99, p. 456].

A surprising contradiction can be noticed in certain institutional documentary environments which, while drawing on the discourse on digital competences that "involve safe and critical use of information society

---

49 ISO 23950: "Information Retrieval (Z39.50): Application Service Definition and Protocol Specification".

50 For example, in YouTube, it is sufficient to recopy this sequence "<iframe width="420" height="315" src="https://www.youtube.com/embed/UcFUXhBL4mA" frameborder="0" allowfullscreen></iframe>" starting from "share >> integrate" (Export in Dailymotion, Share in Vimeo) associated with each video. The src property takes as value a unique permalink identifier.

technologies (IST) and therefore mastery of information and communications technologies (ICT)" [EUR 06], deprive their users of the freedom to organize, contextualize and globalize data that are often free to use. This is all the more astonishing as the digital initiatives of commercial companies[51] successfully implement the interoperability that Berners-Lee wanted to preserve in the Web in terms of simplicity and sharing.

The most recent manifestations of digital libraries, through their unlimited storing capacity and resource availability, are a proof of the maturity and robustness of Web technologies, just like the gigantic digital service YouTube, established in 2005, which grows with 300 h of additional video every minute[52] and today has over one billion users throughout the world.

An emblem for ICT technological power, this world leader in the hosting and online distribution of videos has the characteristic that it offers users various mechanisms for resources appropriation. Consulting/viewing, uploading videos, creating thematic channels, development of specialized applications based on YouTube APIs[53] and simply sharing resources, all these illustrate the attention given by Google, owner of the site, to the diversity of uses. Certainly, this does not paint in rosier colors the fact that such marketing-based strategies of opening to a whole range of uses generate huge revenues from the publicity that frequently precedes the videos distributed.

Despite the technological complexity of the distribution of streaming videos to millions of users, the YouTube platform has maintained elementary solutions for resource sharing (permalink and iframe) that are, for example, widely used on blogs by users with little developed computer skills. This ease in distributing YouTube available resources through various technical environments shows that, irrespective of how users choose to adapt it, the logic of use cannot be checked by either device design or preimplementation of supposed or wished for uses.

---

51 Whose economic survival relies on audience and customer loyalty.
52 Millions of Internet users access the audiovisual sequences and this amounts to several billion views (https://www.youtube.com/yt/press/fr/statistics.html).
53 YouTube Data API (video upload and playlist management), YouTube Analytics API (statistics and popularity metrics) and YouTube Live Streaming API (creation, update and management of live events).

With minor variations, the same Web technologies are instrumenting the online technical documentation devices. The capacity to give free access to the resources they host does not depend on the plasticity of technological interoperability, but rather on the political decisions aimed at bringing use at the level of accessibility.

Today's IR practices are no longer focused exclusively on the fields of research, education or training. All forms of human activity may presently generate a need for information that the individuals will try to meet by searching through countless resources hosted by these sophisticated digital architectures.

And it is only by technological interoperability in the service of use that digital documentary platforms will qualitatively accompany the creation of customized mechanisms, structured to meet specific expectations and approaches.

# Interoperability, Interface and Hypertext

## 2.1. Digital spaces and territories

Boosted by high-performance technical infrastructures and mature Web technologies, large-scale technical documentation architectures have rapidly emerged and have started to shape the global digital landscape. Within several years, governmental initiatives and commercial projects implemented by very large companies have built real digital towers that have become major destinations, prized by millions of Internet users whose virtual activities are organized around countless services and content of all types, continuously updated and systematically improved [AND 12, BAC 09, MUS 08, BER 08, SOU 03b]: "More than ever it should be stressed that the articulation between technology and society movements should not be thought of only at micro-social level (many studies dedicated to uses lead to this approach), as it is important to also consider the manufacturers' strategies as well as the public policies, and to situate the changes that affect information, cultural and communication practices within their long term evolutions" [MIE 04, p. 117].

The development of the digital economy and the electronic transformation of public services have generated major changes in the citizen[1] and

---

1 "A democratic society, at least in the Western sense of the word, makes it possible for every citizen to participate in the public life, to ponder the opinions that determine the future of the society he lives in, to freely express in public, as a space for exchanging arguments and views. This obviously implies that every citizen has access to knowledge about the world around him, in all its dimensions" [BOU 13, p. 10].

consumer[2] behavior. Administrative procedures (health, justice, employment, retirement, income tax, education, etc.) and most of the consumption acts (energy, water, holidays, bank, insurance, equipment, etc.) cannot be handled without digital mediation and inevitably lead to information retrieval (IR) practices, small-scaled as they may be, for functional and household needs [VID 13, TCH 11, BRO 07, WIL 06, CIA 05].

The present Web essentially differs from the initial Web in terms of the topographic dimension conferred by strong identity reference sites, regulated by legal values, shaped by governmental actions and led through ambitious economic strategies [HEN 14, AMB 06, MAT 05, MAT 01]. Browsing and IR practices are no longer applied in a heterogeneous information universe[3] in which precursor search engines such as Altavista, Nomade, Excite, HotBot, etc., struggled to certify quality spaces and reference sources[4] in order to meet the Internet users' demands.

Territories with distinct frontiers emerge in this globalized digital space, and they become places where citizens and organizations really express their societal activities. These digital territories with displayed identities and recognized characteristics are places of controlled digital urbanization[5], which any Internet user-citizen is free to cover, exploration and discovery conditions being, in the end, far better than those that accompanied the first generation Web of documents. In France, from 2010, the Legal and Administrative Information Department (Direction de l'Information Légale et Administrative (DILA)) is in charge of legal dissemination, publishing and administrative information and supervises several institutional

---

2 "The individual wants to become a real 'consumer' in relation with his entrepreneurial interlocutors through stronger involvement in the organization's value chain. He becomes a direct player in the company's commercial policy, as well as its full partner" [DEB 10, p. 10].

3 Public information, scientific and educational information, advertisement information, media information, personal information, etc.

4 "The 'mixture of genres': in the digital environment all documents are, if not "gray" like the cats, at least very similar; and one of the difficulties is related to this first stage when the Internet user has to identify the type of document he deals with: article, extract of a work, blog post, site or webpage?" [SER 05, p. 40].

5 "Access to high-speed Internet has become an essential condition for the access to information, education, training, leisure activities, administrative services" [FRA 08, p.5]; "Access to networks and digital services has become one of the conditions to integrate our economy, society, democracy, culture" [FRA 08, p.7].

information sites dedicated to citizens: boamp.fr (official bulletin for public procurement announcements), bodacc.fr (civil and commercial announcements), info-financiere.fr (centralized storage of regulated information), journal-officiel.gouv.fr (legal and regulatory texts), legifrance.gouv.fr (publishing laws online), vie-publique.fr (public debate), service-public.fr and ladocumentationfrancaise.fr.

The same founding principles stated by Berners-Lee are at work in these digital territories: "Principles such as simplicity and modularity are the stuff of software engineering; decentralization and tolerance are the life and breath of Internet" [BER 98]. Despite their software sophistication, Web browsers continue to propose viewing of hypertext markup language (HTML) formatted textual resource content, present at any point of a Trellis computer network and identified by a network address (uniform resource locator (URL)) that determines the access and repatriation of content (HTTP).

## 2.2. Interactive services

Because of its use and deployment simplicity, the hypertext technological architecture imagined and conceived by Berners-Lee to meet information dissemination needs has become the best candidate for the instrumentation of our "Information and Knowledge Societies". However, this change of scale has introduced the need to complete the initial documentary architecture with functionally collaborative data processing interactive services. The shift from a static conception to a dynamic conception of Websites, where information, extracted from databases, is presented in on-the-fly layout by means of middleware solutions, has become a *de facto* standard (blog, content management system and social networks) [SAL 99].

By introducing its new information processing features, the Web's technological interoperability reached a mature expression of Berners-Lee's founding works without calling into question their purpose in terms of simplicity, modularity, openness and freedom of access. Thus, the significant improvement brought by technological interoperability in regards to processing of data in view of their dissemination on the Web did not seem incompatible with the logic of openness and freedom of access preached by the W3 founder.

Nevertheless, numerous technical documentation architectures dedicated to citizens, caught in the race for greater audience and popularity like all online devices, have finally diverted the interoperability mechanisms by limiting them to a perimeter that called into question the openness and the Internet users' freedom to come and go as they pleased during browsing (Figure 2.1).

This conception calls into question a satisfactory approach of interoperability: "A state which exists between two application entities when, with regard to a specific task, one application entity can accept data from the other and perform that task in an appropriate and satisfactory manner without the need for extra operator intervention" [CEN 99].

The extended functionalities of these online documentary environments, subject to the creation of a user account, are often similar in nature[6]: query and selection backup, alerts, exportation of references, personalization of the inquiry interface, etc. They have no immediate connection with the problematics of personal data confidentiality and might be advantageously made available to everyone due to numerous technical variations linked to Web services and to the infinite possibilities to have modular extensions of the browser[7].

---

6 Creating an account on http://www.revues.org permits us to save the searches conducted with a search engine that is integrated to the OpenEdition site. These searches can be the object of alerts (three at most) sent to the account owner by electronic mail. On http://www.persee.fr, the creation of a personal account permits us to preserve search results, create a library of articles, comment on the articles and associate labels to documents. The functionalities extended on http://www.cairn.info through the personal account are very close to those of Persee.fr. On http:/ww.uoh.fr, opening an account will permit, in a very elementary manner, us to store the favorites and save comments.

7 For example, the tool Zotero (http://www.zotero.org), which was created in 2006, is dedicated to the management of documentary references (not only bibliographic references). This tool does not depend on Web sites, and exists as a standalone application as well as a plugin that extends the possibilities of Web browsers and text processing software (Microsoft Word, LibreOffice, OpenOffice, etc.). It permits us to collect and organize in a very simple manner all the references coming from arXiv, Jstor, Amazon, SUDOC, etc., of all the sites that are compatible with the functioning of Zotero.

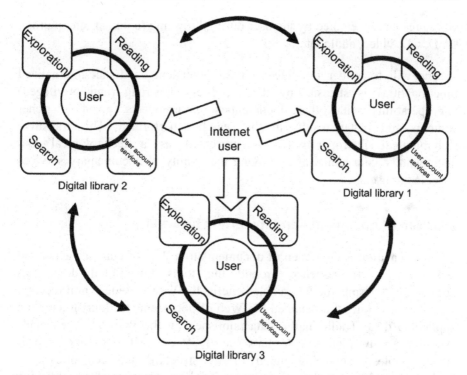

**Figure 2.1.** *Status change. The Internet user who accesses a digital library according to common Web browsing functionalities has his/her user status transformed into a specific user status. Specific iconographies and functionalities that are accessible only to those who have created a user account tend to privatize browsing and limit it to the contents of the documentary platform. The possibility to progressively save the links activation within a digital library, which the browser automatically performs by way of browsing history, are put in check by AJAX programming techniques that are intensively used by these environments. This deactivation of the browsing history in the browser (the Internet user's general path) increases the browsing privatization exercised by the digital library*

These complementary functionalities, conditioned by the creation of a personal account and usable only within a specific digital library environment, are less technically satisfactory than what general search engines (Google, Bing and Yahoo) propose. These facilitate the saving of a history of all the searches (typed words) irrespective of the site viewed, by means of a specific toolbar integrated in the browser. For example, the customized alert mechanisms regularly send the results of automated searches to an e-mail account indicated by the user. As for the export of references, tools such as Zotero can save in XML, under adapted formalism, all the resources retained by the user during browsing (book, article, journal, DVD, CD, video, audio, etc.).

The will to render the Internet user dependent on device-internalized functionalities is stressed by the promises of strong (and privileged) interoperability with other documentary environments, proof of richer contents and better results in the searches performed. This transitive technological interoperability[8] is presented as a technological and documentary gain aimed at improving the quality of documentary services provided to users.

## 2.3. Web of documents and hypertext browsing

The transition from a Web of documents to a Web of data has generated technological effervescence around the tools for digital documents production: "Despite the inarguable benefits the Web provides, until recently the same principles that enabled the Web of documents to flourish have not applied to data. Traditionally, data published on the Web has been made available as raw dumps in formats such CSV or XML, or marked up as HTML tables, sacrificing much of its structure and semantics (…) Underpinning this evolution is a set of best practices for publishing and connecting structured data on the Web known as Linked Data. The adoption of the Linked Data best practices has lead to the extension of the Web with a global data space connecting data from diverse domains" [BIZ 11, p. 205].

Caught up in the tidal wave of radically changing technological innovations, the problematics of usability and cognitive accessibility that scientific works on hypertext and hypermedia reading [ANG 11, ANT 10, CLE 07, BAC 04, DUC 02, ROU 97, BAR 96] had started to highlight were left in the dark. The technological boom has nourished the imaginary of solutions adapted to nascent digital uses and has engaged developers and editors of computerized documentary systems in the validation of coherent use of their devices in the effective service of functionalities expressed in the specifications [WAL 07, PRI 05, PAV 89, PLA 88].

---

8 Mutualization of services and digital funds due to the interoperability of Persee.fr platforms; cairn.info, erudit.org and Armand Colin.

The few use-centered studies on users' appropriation of digital environments give rise, at the most, to certain skepticism, when they are not ignored by the technical solutions designers. Being aware of the constant evolution of technologies they design, they relativize these studies as they consider them out of phase with the very users' demand for improvement.

The "design in use" process advocated by ergonomics psychologists [FOL 03, BEG 00] as a way to confront technical achievements with effective use that is consistent with the needs, either explicit or not, of the users, remains a respectable wish that has hardly been put into practice, notably in the digital libraries design process [CHA 07a, LUP 07, CER 04]. Elaborated without real visibility of use, these digital spaces for documentation are nevertheless a source of problems well known in scientific studies on cognitive and information overload [DIN 08, CHE 05, CAS 96].

In fact, information professionals consider that digital libraries are often a waste of time and money [KUN 96]: the D-Space digital repository installed at Cornell University is a clear illustration [SMI 03]; even though it was designed to enhance scientific research activities, after several years the non-use of the installation is a fact [DAV 07].

Use studies elaborated on the basis of technologies that are inevitably considered obsolete by the Information Technology (IT) teams nourish the certainty that "good technical sense" allows these teams to elaborate adequate solutions for the effective use of these products and tools.

Technological appropriation by the design and development teams has often been done within intranet projects with identifiable use conditions, as they responded to explicit business processes, known organizational structures and determined flows of information: "The list of needs is generally compiled by a group (...) The team in charge with drafting it has to contain at least one representative of the users or sponsors and one technical representative of the development team. As the needs specifications are a contract between these two groups, it is important to see to their fair representation in the team that defines the needs" [CON 00, p. 113].

Though they implement the same technologies as those used in the global Web, these organization-specific information systems are essentially different in terms of complexity and accessibility. When, due to the technological expertise acquired while working on intranet projects [SAL 99, COU 97], these teams participate in the development of technical documentation architectures for open use, in accordance with the Web spirit, they are faced with the need to respond to hardly formalizable browsing and reading practices of a wide community of Internet users[9] whose technical, cognitive, information, etc., profiles are unknown.

Having direct influence on the conditions of production, dissemination, reception and valorization of digital information, this highly normalized technological context of digital documentary objects suggests that uses and digital practices are, in fact, normalized themselves, whatever the vocation of the digital environment used: "The studies on computerization thus appear correlated with the development of technologies that, by transforming the information processing processes, impact the organization of human activities. Driven by the constraints on data processing or rather by the modeling of information exchanges it has stimulated, labor organization forms adapted to computer operation conditions and to human labor shall be implemented" [HOC 06, p. 290].

This is the source of the central question of the relations between technological proposals and their embedded presuppositions in terms of use. The works of Pierre Rabardel [RAB 98, RAB 95] in the field of cognitive psychology have shown that a technical artifact cannot be dissociated from a subject's activity (and its context). Such an artifact, either material or not, identified as a tool by its designers, cannot aspire to a status other than that of a symbolic device, unless an effective instrumental genesis confirms the transformation of the tool in an instrument that serves the subjects' activities and the ends they pursue.

This mutation from a superficial use to effective appropriation of the artifacts reveals the activity of subjects as a form of development of the dimensions of goal achievement and productive task accomplishment that are articulated with the dimensions of elaboration of external and internal resources of the constructive activity (epistemic mediation, pragmatic mediation, reflexive mediation and interpersonal mediation) [FOL 05, CER 04].

---

9 Multicultural, multisite, multilanguage and with highly variable degrees of expertise.

This logic of use endangers the effectiveness of the system paradigm, which is the dominant approach in the great majority of digital technological devices, to the detriment of the user, to whom the functionalities of these devices address. Unusability, unacceptability and even rejection of the digital devices by their users/recipients frequently originate in the logics of use being ignored or insufficiently taken into account during the development process [BAR 07, PAP 07d, PAP 04, GAR 03].

During the establishment of intranets, the users' functions being known and their roles in the organization being identified, the technical solutions deployed are synonyms for effectiveness in terms of their capacity to meet the needs of the organizations and actors involved. When developed in isolation from the users' profiles, motivations and the context of activity, these same solutions and the functionalities they integrate prove to be less adapted or simply rejected: "Designers being themselves expert users of the Web, they have automated certain browsing procedures and therefore are not anymore able to spot the ergonomic problems posed by a Website, even when it was not developed by them. This confirms that the cognitive functioning of designers depends on the way they analyze the task; this also relies on their knowledge of the users' needs. It follows that Websites, whatever their type, are difficult to access and use by Internet users and do not respond to either their needs or cognitive capacities" [CHE 08, p. 193].

The fact that users do not understand the technological choices retained by the design and development team is expressed by a major sanction: non-use [VID 13, BOU 09b, CHE 08]. This fact requires the device being reconsidered from the user's perspective (profile, needs and skills), and within the context in which use and possible interactions with other devices take place. From this point of view, and precisely when they are the result of governmental or institutional programs aimed at wide dissemination of contents, as part of the society's projects[10], digital libraries can no longer be thought of outside the framework of interaction of important players in the technology and economy of the global Web.

---

10 The Plan RE/SO 2007: "The Digital Republic is an information society that is shared by and for everyone. Thus the Plan RE/SO 2007 aims to 'act upon demand' of users and citizens with regard to access to the resources of the information society", see http://archives.internet. gouv.fr/.

With their undeniable technological supremacy and a dissemination power unrivalled by the national technical documentation devices, these documentary architectures built by major Internet players propose extended functionalities that can be mobilized by Internet users in the spirit of Web interoperability, without trying to shape the uses.

This is where the historic works on hypertext, hypermedia and electronic interactivity regain their whole sense and can on the one hand correct the design errors that are due to strongly asserted confidence in technological possibilities, and on the other hand regain awareness of the principles of free browsing in the digital Web spaces, which are not negotiable [MCA 99, BAL 96, LAU 95, PAP 95, NAN 95, SCA 94, NIE 90, NIE 89, ACM 88].

The solutions for data and document reorganization inherited from the anthropocentric approach of hypertext, in which the Internet user is a real player and not a simple pawn in pre-established technical interactions, can contribute to improving Websites of any nature [SHI 06, HUD 03]. Reconsidered here in its conceptual power, hypertext preserves the promises of the original associative access to digital information by inviting the Internet user to reoccupy this reading/rewriting space that the visionaries and designers of the first hypertext systems had glimpsed. This particularism of hypertextual reading is in line with the fact that "in the future man will have to find his way through ever more diversified information, and it seems that this will shape the future not only of the Internet, but also of all the large databases" [BAL 96, p. 87].

## 2.4. The persistence of hypertext

The tools, communication protocols, data formats, etc., that the economic and scientific players[11] of W3 have abundantly produced during several years have hypertext showing only in the address bars of Web browsers. The massively hypertextual functioning of the Web is expressed by the hypertext transfer protocol (HTTP) or HTTPS[12] abbreviations that introduce the URL

---

11 In April 2015, the consortium counted 380 members, among them: CERN, Google Inc., Facebook, Apple Inc., Microsoft Corporation, AT&T, IBM Corporation, CISCO, INRIA, MIT, Hewlett-Packard, University of  Lyon, Orange, Adobe Systems Inc., Stanford University, University of Oxford, NASA, Mozilla Foundation, OCLC, Oracle Corporation, etc. (see http://www.w3.org/Consortium/Member/List).
12 Hypertext transfer protocol (HTTP), Hypertext transfer protocol secure (HTTP).

that Internet users type in order to access the information sites, directories and search engines and other digital services. Hypertext is also dissimulated in the body of webpages, in an abbreviated form reduced to the technical property of an HTML[13] tag, and it makes it possible to build novel virtual networks that are suitable for multiple browsing/reading paths.

Another technical presence of hypertext is so deeply concealed in the technological mysteries of Web applications that it resembles a discrete recognition expressed by researchers, engineers, technicians and Information and Communication Technology (ICTs) experts of this historical contribution to the emergence of our massively connected world. It is a homage paid by XMLHttpRequest[14], one of the technical objects most commonly used in the Web of data. This technical mechanism gives webpages a higher loading fluidity while limiting the modification/updating of certain parts of the documents due to the AJAX[15] and Document Object Model (DOM)[16] functionalities that the JQuery framework[17] made popular among the global community of Web developers (see Table 2.1).

These rare manifestations may seem archeological, considering the evolutive energy of the ICT permanent renewal, which artificially influences the obsolescence process of techniques (tangible or intangible) and services[18]. The digital urbanization of the global Web suggests that this point of view should be reconsidered, as it is contradicted by the interest that

---

13 The tag <a href= #></a> is an anchor tag that supports the mandatory property *hypertext reference* (hyperlink) by stating the Uniform Resource Idenfier (URI) of the resource to which the expression (sequence of characters or image) between the opening and closing tags will be the origin and pretext for activation. The role of this essential tag of Web hypertextuality has progressively evolved toward programming functionalities (<a href="javascript :alert('clic !')">Appeal to a Javascript function</A>) or applicative appeals (<a href="mailto :contact@site.com">Execution of e-mail client software</a>).

14 The XMLHttpRequest Object, W3C, 5 April 2006, available at http://www.w3.org/TR/2006/WD-XMLHttpRequest-20060405/.

15 AJAX (Asynchronous Javascript and XML) is a technological assembly of programming language (Javascript), asynchronous communication protocol (and XMLHttpRequest) and XML formalism that uses (DOM (see http://en.wikipedia.org/wiki/Ajax_(programming).

16 DOM technical reports, available at http://www.w3.org/DOM/DOMTR.

17 jQuery is open source software framework under MIT Licence (see http://jquery.com). The first version of jQuery was launched in August 2006.

18 For example family-dedicated IT, Internet through switched telephone network, ADSL, digital homogenization for all media, distributed IT, high-speed, mobile telephony, Web 2.0, e-commerce, individual equipment, cloud computing, interoperability, etc.

numerous scientific domains[19] continue to have in the hypertext and hypermedia problematics.

```
<!DOCTYPE html>
<html>
<head>
<script src="https://ajax.googleapis.com/ajax/jquery.js"></script>
<script>
$(document).ready(function(){
  $("#b1").click(function(){
    $("#b1").empty().append("<b>Remplace texte du bouton 1</b>.");
  });
  $("#b2").click(function(){
    $("#b2").empty().append("<i>Remplace texte du bouton 2</i>");
  });
});
</script>
</head>

<body>
  <button id="b1">Texte Initial du bouton1</button>
  <button id="b2">Texte Initial du bouton2</button>
</body>
</html>
```

**Table 2.1.** *An HTML page that uses jQuery framework. In this example, a click on the buttons situated in the body of the page <body></body> will update the areas of the text situated between <button></button>. This operation will not reupload the page. Javascript programming of this operation is visible between the header tags <script></script>*

While computer science (engineering and fundamental science) remains the field where research is most frequently conducted, social sciences (information science, cognitive psychology, education, linguistics and semiotics), arts, architecture, law, literature and languages, etc., have largely taken hold of these study objects.

---

19 Computer science (engineering and fundamental science), information sciences, psychology (cognitive psychology), education, linguistics, semiotics, art, literature, law, architecture, medical sciences, science and techniques of sports (STAPS) and physical activities), etc.

## 2.5. Hypertext and hypermedia

Research conducted on the bibliographical base of ABES[20], specifically on the scientific activity revealed by doctoral theses defended in France between 1990 and 2014, reveals a double incentive: first, that of a pluridisciplinary interest that sees the emergence of specific problematizations and questioning, which go beyond IT approaches, and second, a persistence of these problematics in time, which is really surprising when we consider the major attraction exerted by the Internet phenomenon on all the scientific fields since its emergence.

A more in-depth reading of the works on hypertext/hypermedia conducted in the 1990s [BAL 95, DAC 90, ACM 88] shows that the technological paradigm had been explored by multiple IT devices (tangible and/or software) already capable to support multimedia data (e.g. Multicard, KMS, DynaText, Notecard, Intermedia, etc.) and organize them as networks. The particular nature of the equipment deployed and the originality of the data formats adopted [BAR 96, BAP 96, NEW 91] did not allow for the generalization initiated by W3C, several years later, due to its recommendations and to the industrial partners of computer science, electronics and telecommunications, which gave birth to the globalized Internet that we know today.

Nevertheless, except for these generalization and massification conditions, the technical properties of experimental hypertext systems (ErgoLab, MacWeb, Nestor, etc.) or of those already commercialized (Guide, Grif, DynaBook, HyperCard, Toolbook, etc.) gathered the functional principles that the Web deploys today, often in a more trivial manner[21] [DAC 90].

---

20 The site Système Universitaire de DOCumentation (SUDOC) provides free access to a collective French catalog with contributions from libraries of higher education and research institutions. It gathers over 10 million bibliographical notes (http://www.sudoc.abes.fr).
21 Beyond a physical description of hypertext in terms of nodes and links, hypertext systems have shown how technology could be employed (graphical terminals, audio and video peripherals, rapid access storage, etc.) for easy representation of the information associated with intuitive handling by means of user-friendly interfaces. To this end, local solutions that involved only hypertext system developers were adopted in order to respond to practical problems of version control, browsing or cooperation in the hypertexts.

The emergence of the Internet and its growth in power on a global scale within a short period, while generating a spectacular technological shock wave [MUS 10, BER 08], have eclipsed the period when hypertext/hypermedia stagnated due to complex problems posed on the one hand by cognitive and educational issues (disorientation, information overload, cognitive overload, cognitive profile) and on the other hand by problems of organization of wide hypertextual networks, potentially connected, subject to change by their very nature, indefinitely incrementable and produced by numerous designers either manually or in a (semi)automated way (author logics/reader logics) [SOU 03b, PAN 98, ROU 97, GOL 97, MCK 91].

Moreover, hypertext networks enriched by various contributions in an extended collaborative mode [PAP 03b] became the source of subtle and inextricable problems related to copyright and intellectual property to which positive right struggled to find solutions equal to the implications of multi-author and multi-source digital collaboration [HEN 14, SIR 01, AMB 06, PAP 05, AMB 00].

A reading of the summaries of PhD Theses on "hypertexts/hypermedia" highlights problems that are still relevant, referring to hybrid writing (book/hypermedia), digital writing or reading (correlated with the diversity of accessible multimedia objects), script writing (design and organization of narrative material), the interaction tracks in the subjects' activity, reading/writing practices (notes and learning) or the contextualization of information[22] and hypertextualization[23], which are in the best case skillfully avoided, but most often mishandled, by Web technological solutions [PIE 14, YAZ 13, ANG 11, JEA 00, PAN 98, NAN 95].

It is the case of ambitious digital libraries whose conditions of use are totally out of phase with the technological conditions that contributed to their establishment. Not only have the problems of disorientation

---

22 The acquisition of contextual information aimed at completing primary information and/or accompanying the information/cognitive profile of users/readers.

23 The ways of learning how to write are still very linear (academic works, professional writing, gray literature, etc.) and their transposition in a hypertextual form in order to improve use requires a complex hypertextualization process in order to avoid getting a simple electronic page turning device.

and dissatisfaction not been solved by the technologies employed by websites, but the equipment of the information mass has neither improved the location conditions nor facilitated browsing/ exploration.

The fact that technical functionalities offered by digital libraries to their users are often only used infrequently highlights the gap between the designers' evaluation of these devices, which in their view are "properly functioning" (technocentric approach) and the evaluation made by the users of the same devices (anthropocentric approach), who have serious difficulties in bridging the distance between their cognitive activity and the technical functionalities of the devices they are encouraged to integrate in their activities [CHE 08, DIN 08, CHA 07a, ROU 97].

This observation stands for the great majority of digital libraries, which are underused by potential users unless very strong mediation is provided[24]. With these findings in mind, it is not surprising that users of these technical documentation devices are only using the tools associated with the personal account they are encouraged to create in a superficial way [FAR 08, PAP 07a, PAP 07b]. They prefer basic tools (elementary search) and only use advanced tools for searches that require documentary skills they do not possess (query language syntax, lexical diversity, orthographic variation, synonymy, proximity, etc.)[25]: "High quality products, which are very well promoted by their designers and even remarkably supported from an educational point of view, prove to be unusable" [TRI 03].

---

24 Accessible on www.persee.fr in the "About" section: "Beyond the digitization of printed collections of scientific journals and their online dissemination, Persée aims to offer services and tools that allow for an enriched exploitation of documents without the Internet user perceiving a significant gap in comparison with the electronic edition. Thus the Persée portal brings technological gains comparable to those offered by standard journal publishing portals. These gains are reflected by the functionalities offered to the final user".

25 Recent studies show that, in a majority of cases, the queries formulated contain at least two terms (Jansen, Spink, Saracevic, 2000), which is insufficient for representing a need of information. (...) We know that formulating a query with Boolean operators is counter-intuitive for users that are not specifically trained for this approach (Avrahami et Kareev, 1993)..." [SIM 02, p.405].

## 2.6. Browsing paths

The "digital libraries" initiatives are essentially related to patrimonial actions (Gallica[26], Europeana[27], Lisieux Electronic Library, the Virtual Center of Knowledge about Europe, INHA Digital Library, contemporary music portal, Art History Library, etc.). Many operational establishments of organized digital content repositories are connected with university and research fields (Persée, HAL, Erudit, ArchiveSIC, Research Audiovisual Archives, revues.org, CAIRN, CERIMES, etc.).

From an organizational point of view, these autonomous information devices for the acquisition, organization and dissemination of digital content appear in an ambiguous light. While they aim to support higher education and research, like any other university library, their positioning is in reality delicate and their visibility is relative in the already highly sophisticated documentary systems of university libraries [COT 07, PAP 07b].

Computer architectures and viewer interfaces favor IR modes that replicate those used by general search engines (Google, Yahoo, Exalead, etc.) [RIE 06, SIM 08, BEA 02, ASS 02]. These digital libraries thus simplify the IR into a query practice, which potentially guarantees, due to integral search, to find all resources susceptible to meet the user's expectations.

In reality, this approach generates significant noise and provides the user (who often lacks IR competences) with scarce means for organizing his search results. Furthermore, the tools offered by these documentary environments to the Internet users do not allow them to semantically reorganize the results or to make them available to other users, according to an already acquired logic of "2.0" sharing and collaboration [PAP 03a, SOU 03a, SAL 01].

However, the mechanisms for building "virtual networks"[28] are copiously described in the scientific literature related to hypertext and continue to be

---

26    http://gallica2.bnf.fr,    http://europeana.eu,    http://bmlisieux.fr,    http://www.cvce.lu, http:// www.inha.fr, http://www.histoiredesarts.culture.fr.
27 Europeana gathers 26 million documentary objects: 15 million images, 10 million texts (optical character recognition optical character recognition (OCR) scanned), 440,000 audio sequences, 170,000 videos and 7,000 three-dimensional (3D) objects [FRE 13].
28 Assimilated to rewriting operations.

under study [KOS 11, MAD 09, HUS 98, GOL 97, BUR 96, MAR 93, NIE 90]. Naturally, this is not the case for elementary functions attributed to "authors" of dynamic websites, based on content management systems CMS for which there are two coexisting types of clearly identified Internet users: Internet users who view online information and administrators who have the privileges for intranet/Internet site updates (insertion, cancelation, modification of data and documents, access manager).

Regarding these virtual networks elaborated by readers/authors, the matter is to have the capacity to express multiple points of view (associated semantics) on the resources available within one or more interoperable documentary environments [LAU 02, PAR 02]. A reader's hypertext browsing of a set of networked resources is translated in a consultation path that can take the form of a reusable digital document. This consultation path builds through links that the reader activates in the accessed nodes/documents or by means of the interface commands he uses (previous document, associated document(s), similar document(s), searching for chains of characters, history, connected networks, etc.). The accessed nodes/documents come to represent a "point of view" on a given theme. Once they are cleaned up, reorganized and identified (by the author, a community of authors, a team, etc.), the reading paths can then be provided to other readers. They would thus be indefinitely updated by adding/removing resources and semantization of "nodes" and links composing the virtual network [YAZ 13, DAV 99, BAR 96, FRE 95, NAN 93].

These points of view, materialized in the form of reading paths, which can be made available to other readers by the authors/administrators themselves, offer a mode of access to digital resources through information and/or cognitive profiles. It is from the perspective of these author/reader browsing paths, widely studied in the historic works on hypertext, that the appropriation of digital libraries by the users is permitted. They prove to be easy to implement due to XML technologies.

The detailed description of these browsing paths can take the form of a digital document that does not depend on the technical environment and features a normalized, reproducible and sharable grammar (Document Type Definition and XML Schema).

## 2.7. Consultation interfaces in the service of autonomy

The question of access to constantly evolving digital collections that address wide audiences contributes to the problem faced by traditional libraries for a long time. These problem seem to converge with those actually encountered by digital spaces, in particular by the digital libraries. Questioning referring to accessibility, information overload, cognitive load, technological literacy and instrumental skills, device acceptability, relevance attribution, etc., is crucial as it could help crystallize non-use or unusability of technical systems.

The excessive production of primary resources – whether or not gathered in digital libraries – cannot free itself from the economy of descriptive data, the only data capable of transmitting to the automated information systems not only the rules for document organization but also the conditions of technical and human use, in correlation with the user cognitive and information profiles: "There is a triple difficulty [in solving information retrieval problems]: a detailed search requires words to be saved; at the same time, there is a need to go beyond words, that is to consider concepts, which can be expressed in different words – these concepts are themselves highly field- and context-dependant and they evolve in time to the point where any pre-definition based on expert analysis (such as building a thesaurus) is easily proved to be outmoded and unsuited" [LEF 00, p. 225].

Research conducted in cognitive psychology highlights that the selection of relevant information introduces cognitive digressions and information overload situations that prove problematic even expert to Web users. While technology can assist in isolating several pages in the Web's digital universe, the local processing of the page is each individual Internet user's task. Many difficulties in the browsing of digital documents arise from their architecture, which is not adapted (based on a single use model) and is not rendered immediately perceivable.

For example, institutional information (service-public.fr, legifrance.fr, etc.) available online within the framework of governmental actions aimed at the dematerialization of the administration is, however, not cognitively accessible. Browsing through these information sites is, for the ordinary citizen, paradoxically as frustrating as satisfying; while the quality of information is good beyond doubt, the user is often confronted with the difficulty of contextualizing information, to associate it with the enforced legislation, to evaluate its relevance for his search, etc.

While the institution–citizen dialogue can be improved with more user-friendly interfaces, it is equally important to reorganize content on the basis of users' cognitive models [TIJ 03, HOU 92]. Therefore, the objective of semantic interoperability is essential: "In a context of interaction with the citizen, using a thematic path to access documentary resources or services rather than the more traditional path of source or attachment to a particular administrative unit has become essential. In this context, information linked to the conceptual organization and verbal representation of knowledge is fundamental" [HUD 03, p. 135].

While conceptual approaches may prove insufficient for a precise definition of the frameworks of interactions and effective use that would help adapt to any Internet users' expectations[29], a pitfall to be avoided is the production of either a consultation architecture that is so rigid that it can only be used by experts, or a hybrid composition of various use cases that would not find a user audience.

The evolution of Web technologies (data and document formats, DOM, Javascript, Ajax, CSS, etc.), the power of personal computers and the widespread use of high-definition graphic screens now make it possible to find highly flexible solutions for the organization and presentation of data, and no longer requires significant technical expertise, relying on valid results of pluridisciplinary scientific research [PAP 14a, CHA 06b, RIE 06, KOS 06, HAS 04, RAO 96].

## 2.8. Tools for hypertext and tools for Web users

The results of scientific works and studies on the appropriation of hypertext and hypermedia projects finally stress the place that digital technologies should have. The historic research of Vannevar Bush on the NLS/Augment[30], between 1950 and 1962, underlines the important role – though not central – of these technologies, real cognitive orthosis that should

---

29 For digital libraries established following political initiatives, so all concerned citizens, from the younger to the older ones.
30 http://www.dougengelbart.org/about/augment.html.

augment, but not supplement[31], human activity. Despite the sophistication of the new productions and the spectacular character of the achievements[32], it is a matter of entrusting technical environments with the task of automating human actions inspired by intuition, idea, decision, etc. Hypertext accompanies the idea of an instrumentation that remains under the control of its user and its intellectual line: "Hypertext and other electronic information systems overcome human limitations by providing mechanisms for compact storage and rapid retrieval of enormous volumes of textual, numeric and visual data. The importance of the systems lies in their potential capacity to augment and amplify intellect" [MAR 88, p. 70].

Due to the evolution of information technologies and the limitless power of computers, delegating human decisions to technological artifacts tends to become normal even in daily tasks: finding the best price for a service or product, proposing similar or complementary products, finding the quickest route either by car or by public transportation, signaling traffic disruptions, booking a restaurant that offers exclusively regional dishes within a 500 m perimeter, etc.

The model of decision and responsibility promoted by hypertext is precisely opposite to the delegating tendency and it attempts to retain the tools that remain under the user's control and are conducive to "augmenting and amplifying the intellect". Numerous scientific works (psychology, sciences of education, information sciences, semiotics, etc.) have confirmed that disorientation and cognitive problems inevitably encountered by hypertext users are closely linked with the body of information available in the hypertextual networks and to the reading strategies, which are constantly being reconfigured: "It is a well known fact that hypertext exploration poses many problems: loss of orientation, cognitive overload and dissatisfaction (...) One of the reasons advanced by researchers to explain these problems is the limited span of working memory, which would rapidly become saturated with the amount of elements to be retained during information retrieval (actual page, pages visited, pages to visit, position in the hypertextual network, status of the current search, etc.). A further explanation of these problems is related to the difficulty that users encounter when trying

31 Like, for example, those for senses and motor functions: binoculars (or microscope)/prescription glasses, bike/wheelchair, throat microphone/megaphone, etc.
32 Such as 3D devices for the exploration of physical or digital libraries [CUB 08, FEK 06, AND 06].

to have a mental representation of the hypertextual space in which they move".

The solutions proposed for reducing the difficulties of IR in hypertext are directed on the one hand toward the visualization of hypertextual space and on the other hand toward the alternative access to hypertextual reading based on the tree-like structure of the documents with author/reader Trellis hypertext.

These modes of representation and access were integrated into historic prototypes such as MacWeb, Nestor, HyWebMap, etc., and have proved to be easy to use: "One of the objectives of interactive interface development was to give the user the possibility to rely on his/her common sense and knowledge of the world when browsing the abstract field of information. What in the beginning is abstract may become perceivable and be the subject of experience" [ROK 03, p. 113].

Due to the lightning development of the Web of documents, these solutions were outshined by general search engines that imposed an information processing mode on the "questions/answers" pattern. In a context where political, economic and societal stakes were not prominent, if they ever existed, this approach to digital information processing has driven practices to a simplistic mode: "This is why interfaces with general purpose, in terms of content, and universal purpose, in terms of targeted users, are necessary" [MIE 03, p. 29]. Multimedia resources increasingly displayed throughout the global network have put in serious trouble the indexing mechanisms of search engines and this has led to reconsidering the need to dispose of solutions for content exploration and synthetic representation without which resources risk to remain inaccessible in the absence of a description shared by Internet users.

Besides the inescapable input field, the ina.fr site offers the user the possibility to discover digitized videos and sounds, namely around 350,000 documents[33] produced by the French radio and television broadcasting. The information is organized under five classes (themes, personalities, programs,

---

33 40,000 h of images and sounds. Eighty percent of the presented videos and sounds can be consulted online free of charge, in their integrality. The remaining 20% can be consulted free of charge in a proportion of 10% of the resource, which is the first several minutes.

features and Web creations), structured into main categories (for example, themes contain 14 main categories: politics, art and culture, sports, entertainment, science and technology, media, advertising, etc.) and subcategories.

These classes, categories and subcategories can be explored in a very elementary way, going from one level of the hierarchy to another, until reaching the final one, where audiovisual resources are represented [GES 02]. At this level, a hypertextual logic of transversality can be reintroduced for the resources presented in several subcategories. The path followed through categories and subcategories in the tree structure is given by an "Ariadne's thread" (distinct from the history). It is highlighted on the fly in the browsing interface of the Website and shows the user the depth of level he has reached. This Ariadne's thread is itself interactive and permits the user to go back at any moment to a higher level in the tree diagram. These location methods may seem insufficient given the stakes of user browsing and valorization of digital collections. A disoriented Internet user is not only at risk of abandoning current browsing, but also of putting the site into quarantine. These location indications find no place in the websites, except for intrusive approaches, as the majority of Web designers and computer graphic designers perceive them as external constraints that corrupt the original visual and ergonomic identity of their work.

While the tree-like organization tends to reduce the Internet users' drift, additional information on the density of resources at a certain level and on the possible links with other categories of the same level can contribute to a complete browsing (Figure 2.2). It is from now on possible to dynamically generate such graphical representations in order to assist the user in his browsing (Figure 2.3) and to spare his working memory.

These graphical possibilities are natively available in recent browsers that have integrated the most recent recommendations of W3 relative to the cascading style sheet[34] (CSS): "Another advantage of CSS is that aesthetic changes to the graphic design of a document (or hundreds of documents) can

---

34 http://www.w3.org/TR/CSS2/, Cascading Style Sheets Level 2 Revision 1 (CSS 2.1) Specification, W3C Recommendation 07 June 2011.

be applied quickly and easily"[35]. Until the recent past, despite the real interest in the visualization of information (which grew in importance in the operating systems with graphical user interface), the technical complexities of their implementation have prevented them from being commonly used in the websites (Figure 2.4).

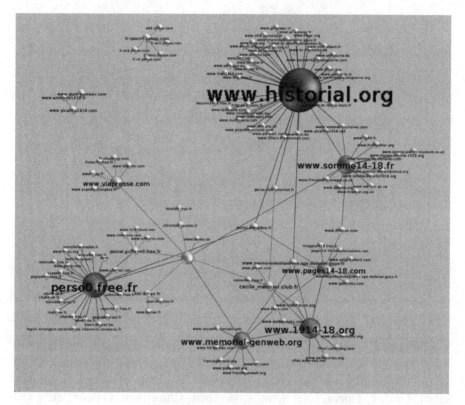

**Figure 2.2.** *One of the numerous representations obtained with GEPHI, an open-source network analysis and visualization software, developed in Java. The application uses a 3D rendering engine, combines integrated functionalities and a flexible architecture in order to explore, analyze, spatialize, filter and regroup all types of networks. While it is not dynamically usable for the Web, processing results can be subjected to interactive exports due to an HTML5/CSS/Javascript combination. The representations generated by GEPHI correspond to an important need to process a huge amount of data available on the Web (data.gouv.fr, www.data.gov) and make hidden properties visible. These visualization tools, complementary to statistical tools, are known to facilitate reasoning and analyses*

---

35 See https://en.wikipedia.org/wiki/Cascading_Style_Sheets.

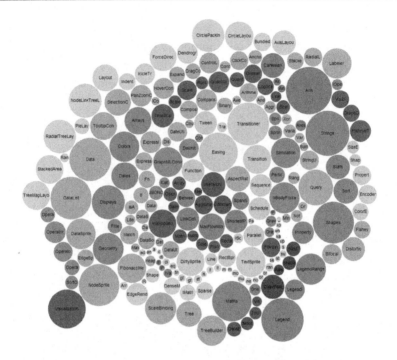

**Figure 2.3.** *A work that essentially uses Javascript and CSS (Jquery). Each circle (here representing a term) is interactive and returns in another part of the interface (not represented here) the list of documents attached*

Elaborated graphical propositions frequently required preliminary installation of additional modules (Java 3D plugin, Flash player and SVG) whose functioning was uncertain, given the available browsers (Explorer, Safari, Firefox, Opera, K-meleon, Konqueror, Chromium, Galeon, etc.) and the IT platforms (Windows, Mac OS, Linux, etc.) (Figure 2.5).

In the case of enterprises present on the global Web, their sites' visual identity and functionalities have to simultaneously distinguish themselves from other sites and avoid exposing the Internet users to browsing comprehension difficulties that may lead them to abandon browsing in favor of a competing site. The designers of these online devices focus their entire intelligence on providing Internet users with the functionalities they commonly use and giving them a sense of originality that will lead them to participate in a novel "User Experience" while interacting with a site which essentially offers the same services as other similar sites. The autonomy of the Internet user–client is subtly revisited in these commercial sites so that he/she is progressively exposed to different browsing projects, led to various places on the site where new products, new services, etc., can be discovered. Ingenious methods are applied to transform initial autonomous browsing into an assisted visit where the risk of disorientation is skillfully eliminated.

**Figure 2.4.** *Example of a word cloud. This visual representation of the words in a document (or a set of documents) gives an idea on their importance (relevance). The more significant the word, the bigger the font. This cloud representation is particularly interesting when term copresence is significant. As copresence calculations may be complex due to the number of documents and terms, they are rarely integrated in the visualization offered by websites, which privilege display immediacy over any other preoccupation*

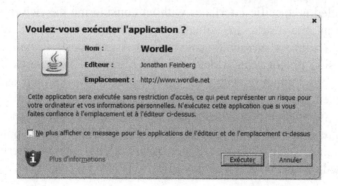

**Figure 2.5.** *A run request issued by a Java virtual machine for the visualization of a word cloud (http://www.wordle.net). Several issues such as security questions, the need to update software versions, numerous bugs in the plugins and applications, etc., have prevented designers from implementing information visualization in websites, which would have improved browsing through websites information space*

In the case of patrimonial, scientific, educational or institutional digital libraries, there is no question of using subterfuges to obtain ownership of the Internet users' browsing. The online resources in these documentary architectures are part of a declared political project of "Society of Information" in which the states make sure that all the information citizens need is being provided and made accessible – all sources being treated equally [KIY 09, ARN 06, MAT 05]. Being concerned by social justice and willing to bridge the digital gap, governments have the obligation to propose information that contributes to everybody improving their quality of life while respecting their rights and duties. A common function of the digital libraries financed by governmental programs is to make their resources accessible so that every individual may use them according to his own culture, capacities, needs, interests and aspirations.

They all valorize content in order to respond to a diversity of expectations, needs and digital practices of the Internet users. This attempt to valorize digital collections should not be assimilated with the excesses of marketing promotion, but rather with the will to meet the Internet users and inform them about the existence of qualified resources that may meet their demands. The use and usability of libraries, archives and repositories can thus be expressed as follows: "With increasing online information sources, users have more and more choices even for a single information task. This substitution effect of different information sources is not well-considered in the design process of digital libraries. User studies of most digital libraries were targeted at specific interfaces without considering the rich information environment the users are situated in and the myriad of competing information sources surrounding them (...) A gap exists in current digital library design practices in which a digital library is disconnected from its targeted user community. Many digital libraries are losing their users; users have learned how to use search engines to access open Web content of collective knowledge of a wider mass, but not digital library content which may require more effort in locating the digital library's entry point. Thus, search engines have disintermediated many digital library interfaces and their related evaluation and usability efforts" [PAN 14, p. 196].

Given their common stakes, these documentary devices should share the modes of organization and description that facilitate the access, reading, extraction and reconstruction of spaces of information and knowledge adapted to the Internet user. By highlighting the power of ICT, digital libraries place themselves in contrast with physical libraries, by discrediting their limited spaces for obsolescence, uncomfortable accessibility and sets of shelves full of bulky works that are difficult to renew [PAN 96]: "A university library can in itself be considered a system that regroups several subsystems of complex information, and in which individuals search through, select, sort out and process information of various natures. Our study aims at responding to a demand addressed by the university library of Metz concerning the reorganization of the existing signaling system. This system is obsolete and insufficient and does not respond to the users' orientation and information needs" [LAL 07, p. 1].

This brutal parallel between the innovative technological features of digital libraries and the physical characteristics of traditional libraries does not place the latter in an advantageous light, though they offer modes of organization of universally shared collections [BEG 05]: "In the interwar period, documentation progressively became a new field of activity in France, in which persons willing to transmit knowledge activate. This new profession, linked to Scientific and Technical Information, emerged as a result of the reasoning, will and sustained action of men and women in the service of knowledge" [MAG 85, p. 5].

Common to all libraries, the fact that works are gathered in a disciplinary field or under the same theme reflects an intellectual or educational project expressed in a cumulative pattern of knowledge. From this reasoned accumulation and conservation of works that form an assembly, structures of meaning are eventually born [JAC 01, NAU 00, BOW 99]. In this sense, the organization of collections reveals the objective projects of knowledge organization carried by the wide classifications instantiated by any library, irrespective of size or nature of its collections: "Classifications are powerful technologies. Embedded in working infrastructures they become relatively invisible without losing any of that power" [BOW 99, p. 319]. Beyond scholarly logic elaborated and used only by the initiated, these intellectual documentary techniques are extremely relevant when going from generic to specific, and vice versa [SAL 72].

Such intellectual methods can be mobilized in the approach of documentary artifacts of digital libraries and could become common tools for exploration and discovery purposes.

As an example, the *Visual Catalog* presents itself as a way to bring specificity and facilitate comprehension of the libraries' plural complexity

(Figures 2.6 and 2.7). Previous to its conception, several features were mentioned as most prominent: the device highlighted the main directions in terms of knowledge organization within the library, revealed the productive proximity of analytical and systematic indexing, facilitated the learning of indexing and classification languages and finally displayed on a unique screen, in a synthetic manner, the global coherence of a system for knowledge organization in order to contribute to the development of real documentary competences concurring to the users' autonomy.

Staging metadata referring to the organization (classification) and descriptions (subject indexing) of the physical and digital resources of the libraries/media libraries, this device attempts to meet the users' needs, among which the capacity to browse the collection of documents while maintaining the global view of structuration: "To be able to take ownership of the information sourced by the collection of documents, the user needs to be provided with the means to comprehend it in its entirety" [TRI 06, p. 15].

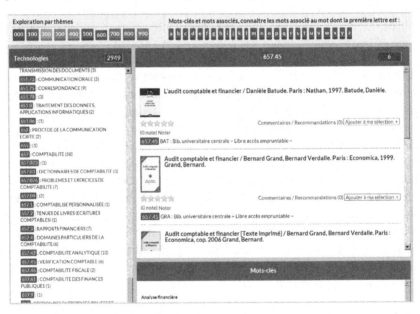

**Figure 2.6.** *Theme-based exploration of the Visual Catalog (http://www.titralog.com). The left column shows all the themes associated with the big divisions of the Dewey Decimal Classification. In this example, it is the "600" division relative to technologies that was selected and it contains 2,949 resources. The upper section of the right column presents the works associated with one of the categories (657.45 "Auditing" counts six works). The lower section mentions all the keywords of the six works under the 657.45 index*

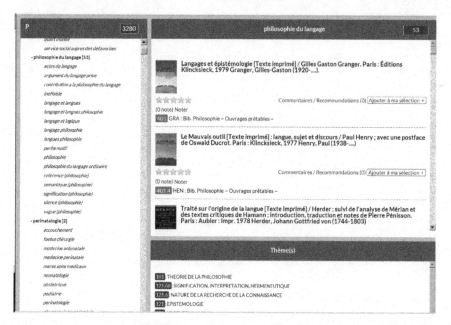

**Figure    2.7.**    *Keyword-based    exploration    of    the    Visual    Catalog (http://www.titralog.com). The left column shows a comprehensive list of all the keywords with a selected initial (here P). The upper section of the right column indicates the works associated with a term. In this example, the term "philosophy of language" specifies 53 resources organized in themes that are shown in the lower framework (theory of philosophy, significance, interpretation, hermeneutics, epistemology, etc.). An exploratory reading, with a tree-based functioning (generic themes and alphabet letters), can change into a transversal and hypertextual reading due to the interactivity of indices of the section "Theme" and the classification marks of each resource*

Today, digital libraries materialize the most remarkable technological advances of a society decidedly orientated toward information and knowledge. The availability and accessibility aimed at by the designers of these sophisticated documentary devices are seriously endangered by the difficulties encountered by the users and shown, though rarely, by pluridisciplinary studies of use. To avoid the situation where an important part of the digital libraries' collections of documents remains unused, similarly to the traditional libraries, it is imperative to stop privileging the technological direction and rethink the design of devices so that they respond to their users' activities.

# Usage-Oriented
# Interoperability Instruments

## 3.1. From computer science to information and communication technologies (ICT), and from ICT to Web technologies

Web technologies have facilitated the development of publication sites with elegant graphic design, intuitive semiotics, refined interactivity, infallible availability, guaranteed evolutivity, which are completely compatible with the habits of users accustomed to the social Web. The earliest versions of HyperText Markup Language (HTML), which historical publishers (Microsoft and Netscape) transformed as they saw fit[1] to ensure a "captive" audience, have given way to much more structured versions, conforming to the recommendations of the W3 (HTML 4.01, eXtensible HyperText Markup Language (XHTML) and HTML5). These versions, implemented in the latest-generation browsers (Chrome, Safari, Firefox, Opera, etc.), are stricter from a syntactical viewpoint. Inspired by Extensible Markup Language (XML), they extend the separation of the logical structuring of content and the formatting properties.

For all actors, being able to draw upon this vast field of stabilized technologies lends them the confidence to employ a generalized mode of operation of active dissemination of information – professional, institutional, cultural, social information, etc. Beyond their initial informational

---

1 An example is the <frameset></frameset> tags and the JavaScript language introduced by Netscape. The frameset tags were completely eliminated from HTML5, so recent versions of browsers such as Chrome and Opera no longer display them.

orientation, the myriad Web technologies are nevertheless computer technologies, which integrate flexibly into the dynamic model of our networked societies, and are capable of more easily reintegrating the complex procedures of computer technology of former times.

The appearance, throughout the world, in the space of only a few years, of millions of Websites (both Internet and Intranet) has helped improve the operational nature of these technologies and lent them a great deal of credibility. A further effect of the proliferation of Websites, which is indicative of the evident domestication of these technologies by a very large number of people, was to alter the status of these technologies, meaning they were no longer the exclusive preserve of experts and specialists in (highly) scientific and technical computing, attaching them to the broader domain of communication.

The worldwide availability of linked digital information services, constantly accessible from any connected site in the world, has led to the construction, in users' minds, of the idea of high-performing technologies – reliable, robust and easy to use. The sprawling reality of these technologies, repositioned in the world of the everyday, has gone hand-in-hand with partisan discourse, transmitted by mass media, conveying a positive and modern image of such technology.

It could even be said that this form of technological instrumentation offers a new strategic dynamic. By agreeing to convert not only their information system but also the whole organization of the working process (workflow and groupware) to operate with these new instruments, organizations have reaped the benefits of controlled porosity between the internal and external environments (the latter including customers, partners, subsidiaries, etc.) who are increasingly excited by those same technological instruments: "In times past, certain economic actors were able to put off the implementation of technologies for a long time, or even avoid it completely without any major risk to their long-term survival. Today, those same actors – for fear of disappearing – cannot possibly avoid the necessity to integrate Internet technologies into their working environment" [GER 01, p. 63].

These phenomena – which pertain at once to media, technology, culture and social aspects – because of the incessant repetition of technological discourse correlating to the rise of global economic competition, have ultimately rendered techno-informational applications and architectures invisible, while at the same time expanding their orthetic omnipresence in both private and professional uses.

The efficiency of these technologies even facilitates the creation of permanent virtual worlds. Such worlds blur the line between the real, unreal and virtual[2], capture the imagination and ultimately obscure the essentially computer-based technological realities of these sophisticated platforms: "Since the accelerated development of the Internet, during the 1980s, contemporary thinking has had difficulty in comprehending the multiple aspects of this new object which, like all communication instruments– which are also instruments of power – produces multiple effects, ranging from fascinating seduction to respectful concern, and many wonderful things in between" [PAR 07, p. 10].

Until recently, to suggest any proximity between the instrumental realities created by Web technologies and the world of the imaginary and fantasy would undoubtedly have attracted scorn. Today, the level of maturity reached by computer technology – both in terms of hardware and of software, the extreme power of the processors in even the lowliest desktop machine[3], the speed of telecom networks, means that Net-connected services are universally available, within everybody's reach. Web technologies can be used to link these services together to serve large-audience distributed computer applications, which would have been inconceivable only a few years ago. Complex online activities, such as the ability to lend permanent, interactive virtual reality to immaterial objects produced by the imagination of thousands of Internet surfers/users, without the need for any computing skill, illustrate the difficulty of preventing the imagination from running wild when we think about using these uniting digital technologies.

---

2 "At present, there are over 300 virtual universes in the world, catering to an estimated total of 300 million Internet users and 50 million phone-based users (...) Companies attempt to harvest knowledge produced by the users via these immersive 3D technological platforms. Thus, a clothes manufacturer can see avatars modeling their range of products in a virtual world, study the outfits which look best together, and offer personalized recommendations which would then be sold in real-world shops" [QUI 08].
3 Grid computing structures such as Desktop Grids group together delocalized and unused computer resources to form a single virtual infrastructure. Modern processors are generally used at less than 20% of their true capacity (e.g. Décryptonand World Community Grid).

Today, any Website development project, whatever its objective, is within the range of the near-unlimited potential of the underlying technologies. Developers dream of a site capable of anticipating visitors' expectations and providing them with a new environment, distinct from the competitors' sites, able to seduce them and encourage them to visit again by way of personalized services.

## 3.2. Digital roaming and the social Web

Since the documentary explosion of the Web, we have seen a constant increase in the use of ICT in a broad sector of human activity – private, public, personal, familial or professional. In November 2013, the *Centre de Recherche pour l'Etude et l'Observation des Conditions de vie* (CREDOC – Living Conditions Research Center) published a report on the spread of ICT within French society. This document, backed up by numerous statistics, shows that 78% of the population have both a landline telephone and a home Internet subscription, and 83% of respondents have a computer at home. Furthermore, in regard to the professional sphere, 54% of those in work have Internet access at work and 50% use the Internet at work for personal purposes.

The omnipresence of Web technologies is such that they now form a fundamental functional infrastructure, which is sufficiently robust to support or even extend a great many human activities. The Web 2.0 approach highlights the Web's significant evolution since its earliest days. In the view of Tim O'Reilly – the originator of Web 2.0 – the concept is organized around seven main principles[4]:

– the Web as a platform;

– harnessing collective intelligence;

– data are the next Intel inside;

---

4 The expression "Web 2.0" refers to a new generation of highly design-oriented Web applications. Web 2.0 has broken away from the earliest technical versions of the Web, evolving into a contribution-based Web. It shows the switch from vertical communication, peculiar to traditional media, to horizontal, "many-to-many" communication [ORE 05].

– end of the software release cycle;

– lightweight programming models;

– software above the level of the single device;

– rich user experiences.

Facebook, Wikipedia, Google, YouTube, eBay, Myspace, Blogger, Delicious, Technorati, Flickr, Meetic, etc., are "Websites/digital environments" which bring together hundreds of millions of users through Web technologies, which are becoming ever less visible and ever more closely associated with social activities[5] [SEM 03, DUB 01]. The first principle, whereby the Web is the foundation for all human activities linked to Web 2.0, highlights the extremely important role played by data, even surpassing that of computer applications. Centralized computer architectures (known as *mainframes*) have given way to distributed architectures (client/server), which have become widespread with the couple "Web client/Web server".

While digital technologies are indissociable from the social phenomenon which is Web 2.0, the techno-centered dynamic[6] of recent years has given way to an anthropocentric approach, whereby users – individually or collectively – are placed at the center of the technical devices. Yet, this approach alone does not mean that the applications delivered by the design and development process will immediately be able to be manipulated by users, but it is indicative of the noticeable transformation in design methods. Indeed, these methods are beginning to integrate the concept of use and cognitive profile of the future users and the social and professional use context [DIN 08, DEN 06, DIN 02].

---

5 As of the second quarter of 2015, the social network Facebook alone had 1.49 billion monthly active users (more than 800 million of whom use the service through their mobiles).
6 The processes of computerization in businesses illustrate this techno-centered dynamic. Following a functional analysis of the processes of information management in business, new computer-based tools are introduced, and the administrative and technical procedures are redefined. Then, the staff are trained to be able to take full advantage of the new computer system and respect the terms of use in accordance with the new procedures.

The profusion of *Open Source*[7] programs, regularly fed by an international community of developers, enriched by the experiences of users who actively contributed to the technical and ergonomic improvement of the devices, is indicative of the flexibility and efficiency of these programming models, which are increasingly widespread in the area of Web development. While these lightweight programming models have had a crucial effect on the realization of robust and usable software tools, they have contributed to the downfall of proprietary applicative logics by ensuring the data are independent of the processing operations. The coherent multitude of document formats inspired by XML has catalyzed the applicative interoperability desired by the W3 Consortium, and represents a significant step in the permanent separation of data and applications.

Regardless of the popularity of these new social digital environments in Web 2.0, the technical mechanisms used for addressing their documentary objects are still those of the Internet. In this sense, they exert no particular constraints on the target objects. Thus, resources of heterogeneous nature and different formats can be linked together to make the Web a truly hypermedia space. Depending on the user settings, Web browsers are capable of immediately reading the most widespread formats (HTML, dynamic hypertext markup language (DHTML), XHTML, cascading style sheet (CSS), graphic interchange format (GIF), joint photographic expert group (JPG), portable network group (PNG), etc.). "Lego®" logic has gradually become more widespread in the implementation of recent Web browsers. Thus, there are infinite possibilities of "reading" any new document format by building a dedicated read module for that format into the browser. Modules specifically developed by the software publishers can be integrated into the browser to execute Flash sequences, read Portable Document Format (PDF) files, view videos in OGG format, listen to audio in MP4 format, interpret Scalable Vector Graphic (SVG) documents, etc.

---

7 The Website *sourceforge.net* offers over 200,000 applications for download. Apache, MySQL, the numerous releases of Linux, Firefox, Filezilla, Gimp, VLC, OpenOffice, AbiWord, NVU, Audacity, etc., are a few of the most widely-used Open-Source applications (client and server) the world over. These applications are not solely for personal and pleasure-seeking uses. Numerous commercial sites make full use of these Open-Source technologies. Thus the providers of mutalized sites and dedicated servers intensively use *Open Source* server applications to configure their material (Linux, FreeBSD, Ubuntu, Apache, Tomcat, Cocoon, MySQL, PostGres, PHP, etc.).

## 3.3. Instrumentation of digital libraries using Web technologies

From the publication language HTML, which is used to organize documentary resources on the Web, to the social and participative model of Web 2.0 [CHI 08, GAZ 08, COH 07, GER 06], the past 15 years have seen an astonishing change. Openly technological at its beginnings, this evolution rapidly became a worldwide social and cultural phenomenon. The essentially IT-based considerations of the rollout of the Internet and interconnection of networks (IEEE 802.3, TCP/IP), which are still just as essential as they ever were, have moved from the foreground to the background. Instead, the foreground now belongs to the more-evolved services designed for users familiar with computer tools, employing various remote communications protocols (simple message transfer protocol (SMTP), network newsgroup transfer protocol (NNTP), file transfer protocol (FTP), hypertext transfer protocol (HTTP), etc.).

The popular phenomenal wave of low-tech online publishing on the World Wide Web – a global network of electronic information dissemination – has given rise to the widespread use of HTTP (Table 3.1) as a default protocol to serve types of communications which were previously associated with specific protocols (post office protocol (POP), SMTP, FTP, etc.)[8] [LEV 98]. The first users of Internet services (messaging, file transfer, file sharing, remote control, document downloading, information searching, etc.) installed on their computers the client applications (often in text or semi-graphical mode) designed to interact specifically with Internet services such as wide area information servers (WAIS), GOPHER, network file system (NFS), Telnet, remote procedure call (RPC), etc.

Although, in the space of only a few hours, we can master the HTML tags used to create electronic documents compatible with the conditions of online publication, the emergence of HTML editors which are often WYSIWYG[9] (and free) has meant that such learning is non-essential, if not actually pointless. Quite quickly, we have come to the point where the

---

8 These protocols have not disappeared, but instead are masked by applications exploiting HTTP. Webmail applications, for example, dispense with the installation of messaging programs on a computer (e.g. Outlook, Thunderbird, etc.) and allow the download/upload of files.

9 Acronym for "What You See Is What You Get".

creation of digital documents[10] for publication on the World Wide Web, combining text and image, no longer requires a great deal of technical skill.

```
GET index.html HTTP/1.1

Host: digital.library.edu

User-Agent:  Mozilla/5.0  (Windows;  Windows  NT  6.1;  Fr-fr;  rv:1.9.1.5)
Gecko/20091102 Firefox/3.5.5 (.NET CLR 3.5.30729)

Accept: text/html,application/xhtml+xml,application/xml;q=0.9,*/*;q=0.8

Accept-Language: Fr-fr,en;q=0.5

Accept-Encoding: gzip,deflate

Accept-Charset: ISO-8859-1,utf-8;q=0.7,*;q=0.7

Keep-Alive: 300

Connection: keep-alive

Cookie: PHPSESSID=4yA7_mP9HgFQSEvbsjfr

Pragma: no-cache

Cache-Control: no-cache
```

**Table 3.1.** *The headers of HTTP 1.1. The page index.html (GET) is requested from the machine digital.library.edu. Upon receiving that GET request, the addressee server sends back the desired document, accompanied by a specific header (HTTP Response)*

A good knowledge of a "text-processing" program improves users' technical skills in online publication, because it makes it easy to convert documents into HTML format. The online microeditors that best exploit CSS and JavaScript, which are now mature, have ultimately implemented this mechanism. The formatting (at least typographical) of blog entries and wiki content has popularized the use of such microeditors. Today, more sophisticated versions – veritable online office suites[11] – which are often free, have made tools for working with text, images, tables, databases and slideshows universally available. Thus, the complex documents (heterogeneous and hypertextual) created by users online enjoy a multitude of export formats.

The mechanisms of technological interoperability have followed the same simplifying evolutionary path. Versions of interapplication exchanges which are more flexible and easier to roll out than Web Services have emerged. The architectures Representational State Transfer (REST) and asynchronous

---

10 Until recently, the expression "electronic document" was still widely used.
11 Examples are OpenGOO, Soho, Google Apps, Microsoft Office Live, Zimbra, etc. These applications may use all or part of Java, PHP, JavaScript, AJAX, etc.

JavaScript and XML (AJAX) revisited and simplified the complex interapplication exchange procedures based on SOAP, UDDI and WSDL[12] (Figure 3.1).

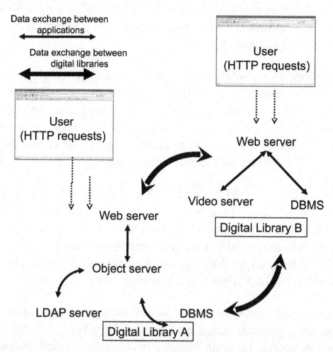

**Figure 3.1.** *Interoperability between digital libraries. The technical architectures of the two digital libraries are different. Digital library B serves audiovisual (AV) resources (e.g. ina.fr, cerimes.fr, canal-u.tv, etc.) whereas library A essentially serves textual resources (persee.fr, cairn.info, revues.org, etc.). Each library is based on a collection of applications working together (four applications in the case of library A, and three in the case of library B), which exchange data with one another through Web services, and ultimately compile those data into a single feed (middleware) to be sent to the user's Web browser. Each digital library is independent, and responds differently to requests from different Internet users. As we might imagine, there is a means of collaboration between the two digital libraries (using the protocol OAI-PMH). A request made by a user to library A might require the momentary cooperation of library B (e.g. linking a video to an article). The user will remain entirely ignorant of this interoperability between A and B. In his/her eyes, the data stream she/he receives will come solely from the library to which she/he made the request*

12 SOAP: Simple Object Access Protocol (message exchanges in XML format between distant objects), UDDI: Universal Description Discovery and Integration (directory of services based on XML), WSDL: Web Services Description Language (XML description of Web services).

These two software architectures constitute a technological compromise, between the need for data processing and an activity of active consultation/reading of resources online. REST and AJAX provide Internet users with the mechanisms to manipulate resources, in line with the usual operations of information-seeking, such as searching, selection, transformation and integration.

These technological solutions can quite easily be employed in digital libraries – as the complexity of these architectures is not even remotely comparable to that of the Web Services – which must, first, supplement their interoperability services with technical response mechanisms compatible with one or other of these two architectures, and second, render visible the structure of the resources offered by the techno-documentary platform (see Figure 3.2).

These architectures – REST and AJAX – are based on the underlying architectural foundations of the Web (identification, interaction and formats) and encourage data exchanges in XML format between numerous online platforms. REST is typically used between machines and servers, while AJAX tends to be used in Web browsers employing frameworks[13] such as JQuery, ASP.NET AJAX, Prototype, Mootools, etc.

With AJAX, the "Internaut" can, in a Web page, embed data extracted from remote environments which are capable of this type of transaction. This data extraction cannot be done blindly, because all asynchronous requests transmitted receive a response in the form of a structured data stream in javascript object notation (JSON), XML or comma-separated values (CSV) format. In addition, these extractions are subject to authorization in the remote environments. For security reasons, Web servers must be informed[14] of requests originating from a different domain. The cross-origin resource sharing (CORS) recommendation from the W3 reflects this requirement, which is implemented in the vast majority of Web servers by the directive "Access-Control-Allow-Origin"[15].

The syndication of really simple syndication (RSS) feeds represents a conclusive action in the area of a technological interoperability, which is often entrusted to content-syndication platforms. In spite of their popularity,

---

13 https://en.wikipedia.org/wiki/List_of_Ajax_frameworks.
14 W3C Recommendation 16 January 2014, http://www.w3.org/TR/cors/.
15 This expression: "Access-Control-Allow-Origin: *" means that any request coming from any domain will be accepted by the Web server.

these online environments impose new usage logics on the Internauts, by way of the procedures and services which come with the elementary function of content syndication.

With AJAX, the syndication of RSS feeds can be done in a variety of different ways, facilitating the creation of original and easy-to-use tools, not hampering the Internaut's initial activity by the imposition of technical logics.

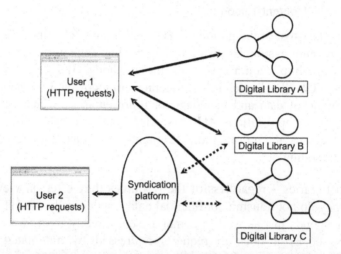

**Figure 3.2.** *Revisited interoperability between the digital libraries and the user. In these scenarios, the aim is no longer to enable the digital libraries to work together independently of the Internaut's requests (the technical means of interoperability within each digital library are preserved). The user can manage the collection and organization of the data extracted from the digital libraries, either head on (scenario of user 1) or by delegation to a content syndication platform (scenario adopted by user 2). The technological processes employed in both scenarios are based on the same mechanisms: HTTP, XML, JavaScript, AJAX, DTD, XSLT, DOM, CSS, etc.*

## 3.4. Architectural invariants of digital libraries

The World Wide Web is an informational space that has historically been organized around three architectural invariants, which are also employed in digital libraries:

1) Identification. URIs (Uniform Resource Identifiers) are used to identify resources and possible convey processing parameters (examples include http://digital.library.edu/index.html and http://digital.library.edu/cgi/getdata. cgi?id=sx234).

2) Interaction. Web applications communicate with one another using standardized protocols which facilitate interactions by the exchange of structured information, with pre-established syntax and semantics. When a URI is entered from a browser or a programming script (Curl, PHP Hypertext Processor (PHP), JavaScript, etc.), an HTTP GET (or HTTP POST) request is sent across the network (and the routing of that request is handled by the Domain Name Service). Once the request is delivered to the addressee, the application server sends the data back in the expected form (Content-Type/Content-Encoding).

3) Formats. Most of the protocols (HTTP, SMTP, FTP, NNTP, etc.) used for recovery and/or submission of representation employ certain methods. The protocol "http" commonly uses the methods GET, HEAD, POST, OPTIONS, CONNECT, etc. Taken together, protocols and methods form a certain volume of data and metadata for representation, which is used for transfer between applications. HTTP sends a simple bit stream along with metadata. It uses the information "Content-Type" and the header fields "Content-Encoding".

Digital libraries – regardless of the resources they offer, in view of the fact that they do not transmit confidential data – specifically use HTTP. This protocol responds just as well to demands sent directly from an Internaut's Web browser as it does to requests addressed by automated content ("scripts") carrying out multiple processing operations on the garnered data. Online RSS-feed syndication platforms work on the basis of this principle. Even when users are logged out of the account which they normally use to update their data, the platform can continue to update the RSS feeds multiple times every day. In place of the user, the platform substitutes a script which carries out the updating operations.

## 3.5. HTML for the Web of documents, XML for the Web of data

Drawing inspiration from the structured language[16] (Standard Generalized Markup Language) [HEW 90], Tim Berners-Lee defined a data-description language which enables authors to use low-level editing tools (ASCII editors) to create textual documents that can quickly be viewed on peripheral devices with different display settings.

---

16 ISO 8879:1986 standard – SGML.

The few dozen (pairs of) tags in the first version of HTML condensed material formatting and logical tagging. The tag pair <H1>...</H1> (Heading 1) identified the title of the page and gave it meaningful visual formatting (large bold characters followed by a blank line on graphic terminals) (see Figure 3.3). This HTML structure is still used today, although Web browsers are capable of reproducing other types of documents (ASCII, GIF, JPG and PNG, among others). With later versions of HTML[17], the material formatting characteristics carried by the tags have gradually been minimized, with the control of those features instead being included on CSSs[18].

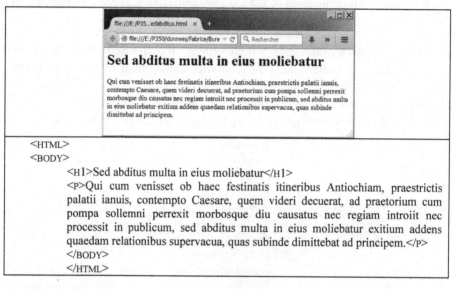

```
<HTML>
<BODY>
    <H1>Sed abditus multa in eius moliebatur</H1>
    <P>Qui cum venisset ob haec festinatis itineribus Antiochiam, praestrictis
    palatii ianuis, contempto Caesare, quem videri decuerat, ad praetorium cum
    pompa sollemni perrexit morbosque diu causatus nec regiam introiit nec
    processit in publicum, sed abditus multa in eius moliebatur exitium addens
    quaedam relationibus supervacua, quas subinde dimittebat ad principem.</P>
    </BODY>
</HTML>
```

**Figure 3.3.** *Formatting in Firefox of a text tagged with HTML version 1.0. The "logical-physical" tags <h1> and <p> are among the few elementary HTML tags recognized by all browser versions (Lynx, Mosaic, Netscape Navigator, etc.). The former (<h1>) assigns the identity of "document title" (header 1) to the tagged portion of text, and in graphical browsers, imposes formatting which is semiotically consistent with the idea of the document title. The latter tag (<p>) attributes a homogeneous presentation on all the sentences within the same paragraph. HTML files are supposed to conform to the tree-like organization of structured documents. However, certain unary tags may interfere with this principle: examples include <img>,<br>, <hr>,<a name>, etc.*

---

17 HTML 1.0, 3.2, 4.0, 4.01, 5.0, and the XML reformulations of HTML, with XHTML 1.0, 1.1, 1.1 and 2.0 highlight the numerous evolutions which the tagging language developed by Tim Berners-Lee has undergone.
18 http://www.w3.org/Style/CSS/.

The tendency to separate the logical structural elements of a text (title, subtitle, paragraph, lists, citations, etc.) from their material forms of presentation (font, size, spacing, color, alignment, etc.) is now in keeping with the principles of the documentary standards SGML and Document Style Semantics and Specification Language[19] (DSSSL). While SGML has brought about high-performing industrial software (Dynatext, Framemaker, Grif, etc.) and has had a concrete impact on the creation of XML and the various versions of HTML, the DSSSL standard has not been implemented on a large scale, with the exception of a few experimental projects such as James Clark's system, Jade[20]. The principles of DSSSL, though, have survived, and appear as the precursor of Extensible Stylesheet Language (XSL).

The normative changes which have transformed HTML have homogenized and limited the idiosyncratic shifts made by Microsoft and Netscape to the tagging language, accumulating a "captive" audience of Internauts (and Web page designers) for the formatting functions in their respective Web browsers (Internet Explorer and Netscape Navigator)[21].

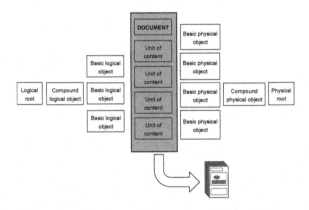

**Figure 3.4.** *Logical structure and physical structure involved in the elaboration of a document. The final document, created for an output peripheral device, corresponds to the collective sum of all the logical elements (title, subtitle, paragraph, list, citation, etc., on the left-hand side of the center element in the figure), with particular typographical and formatting characteristics (on the right-hand side of the center element in the figure)*

---

19 ISO/IEC 10179:1996.

20 http://www.jclark.com/jade/.

21 <blink> (makes the text flash or "blink" in Netscape Navigator), <marquee> (produces a scrolling banner in Microsoft Internet Explorer), <ilayer> and <bgsound> are some of the HTML tags considered to be non-standard.

With the multitude of viewing supports and the increasing role played by digital Audio Visual (AV) resources, this normative evolution has cast doubt on the need for historical tags, marked by a representation inherited from paper publish (articles and books) (see Figure 3.4). Thus, HTML5 introduced numerous tags which essentially pertain to the overall structuring of the resource (<section>,<header>,<nav>,<article>,<main>, etc.) and allow a great deal of freedom for the resources to take proteiform diversity (see Figures 3.5 and 3.6).

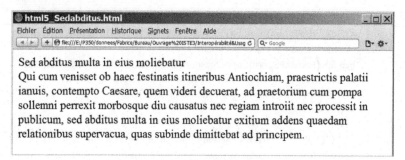

```
<HTML>
    <BODY>
        <SECTION>
        <HEADER>
            Sed abditus multa in eius moliebatur
        </HEADER>
        <ARTICLE>
            Qui cum venisset ob haec festinatis itineribus Antiochiam, praestrictis
            palatii ianuis, contempto Caesare, quem videri decuerat, ad praetorium cum
            pompa sollemni perrexit morbosque diu causatus nec regiam introiit nec
            processit in publicum, sed abditus multa in eius moliebatur exitium addens
            quaedam relationibus supervacua, quas subinde dimittebat ad principem.
        </ARTICLE>
        </SECTION>
    </BODY>
</HTML>
```

**Figure 3.5.** *Formatting of an HTML5 document. This latest release of HTML was the subject of a recommendation from the W3 in October 2014. It places the emphasis on the dimension of authorship and interoperability. The tags <section>, <header> and <article> have no visual effect (apart from a line break after the tag <header>)*

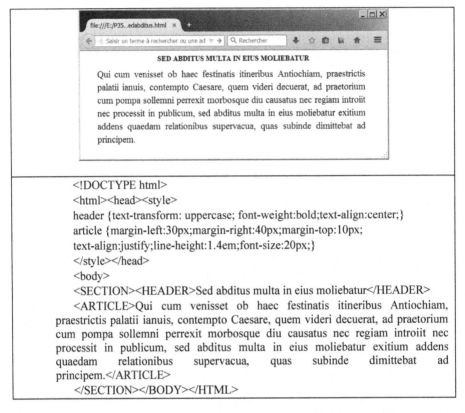

**Figure 3.6.** *CSS formatting of an HTML5 document on the document organization tags. The formatting properties are indicated in the head of the document, between the <head> and </head> tags. The content of the tag <header> will be rendered in capital letters (text-transform:uppercase), in bold (font-weight:bold) and will be centered (text-align:center). The content of the tag <article> is also subject to particular properties pertaining to the margins – top (margin-top:10px), left (margin-left:30px) and right (margin-right:40px). The text will be justified (text-align:justify) and the line spacing slightly increased (line-height:1.4em)*

The irreversible evolution from the documentary Web to the data Web is reflected in the way in which Web browsers work. While their most eagerly-awaited function has proved to be the interpretation and viewing of HTML documents, browsers have also become interpreters of XML documents. They act as XML parsers, and check that the documents correspond to correct syntax to be well formed:

1) XML documents must begin with an XML declaration (of the type <?xml version="1.0" encoding="UTF-8"?>).

2) XML documents must strictly be arborescent and have only one root element.

3) XML elements must have a closing tag ().

4) Tags are case-sensitive (the tag </SECTION> does not close the tag <section>).

5) The XML elements must be correctly positioned (no overlapping or inclusion); (as with HTML, the first opening tag corresponds to the last closing tag. An overlap in the form <section><article></section></ article> yields an invalid XML expression).

6) The values of XML attributes – numerical, alphabetical or alphanumerical – must be enclosed in inverted commas (or dactylographic apostrophes)… e.g.<section id="10" lang=en>.

7) Entities must be used for special characters (e.g. &quot; &amp; & #160; etc.).

With recent browsers, it is possible to combine XML descriptions with CSS styling. This improves the interoperability of all the digital resource distribution platforms. It means that when data are harvested by another techno-documentary architecture, the viewing requests will not run into problems due to displaying behaviors built into the structural entities of the resources.

France's digital topical university portal[22], which syndicates the content of a number of different academic portals, illustrates the advantages of such separation between the logical description of the resources and their physical representation. Each topical academic portal has its own graphical charter and specific descriptions pertaining to the resources it offers. The AV teaching resources of the *Université Digital Juridique Francophone*, the *Université Digital Thématique en Economie et Gestion* and the *Université Ingénierie et Technologies* are organized in a way which is, ultimately, very similar (introduction, search, consultation of a resource, etc.). In spite of this structural similarity, each topical portal has its own visual identity and original presentation models. The harvesting (open archives initiative protocol for metadata harvesting (OAI-PMH)) by the syndication portal from these specialty portals essentially pertains to the logical descriptions of the resources, irrespective of their presentation properties.

---

22 http://www.france-universite-numerique.fr.

Figure 3.7 illustrates the mechanism of externalization of the display characteristics of a native XML document into a distinct style sheet (css.css). Within the XML document itself, the relation with that style sheet will be specified: <?xml-stylesheet type="text/css" href="xmlcss.css"?>.

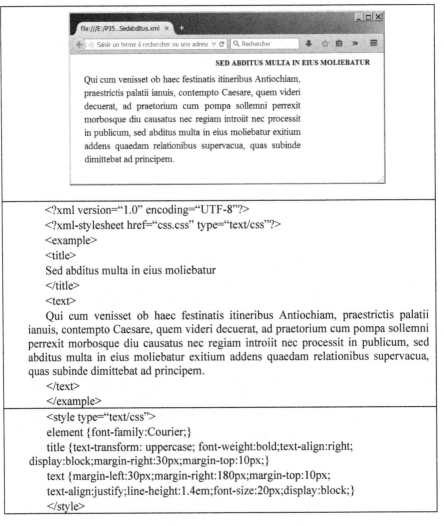

```
<?xml version="1.0" encoding="UTF-8"?>
<?xml-stylesheet href="css.css" type="text/css"?>
<example>
<title>
Sed abditus multa in eius moliebatur
</title>
<text>
Qui cum venisset ob haec festinatis itineribus Antiochiam, praestrictis palatii ianuis, contempto Caesare, quem videri decuerat, ad praetorium cum pompa sollemni perrexit morbosque diu causatus nec regiam introiit nec processit in publicum, sed abditus multa in eius moliebatur exitium addens quaedam relationibus supervacua, quas subinde dimittebat ad principem.
</text>
</example>
```

```
<style type="text/css">
element {font-family:Courier;}
title {text-transform: uppercase; font-weight:bold;text-align:right;
display:block;margin-right:30px;margin-top:10px;}
text {margin-left:30px;margin-right:180px;margin-top:10px;
text-align:justify;line-height:1.4em;font-size:20px;display:block;}
</style>
```

**Figure 3.7.** *Combination of CSS formatting with a well-formed XML document. The XML document is made of an elementary tree structure; the highest level root (<example>) has two offspring (<title> and <text>). The second line of the document indicates the type and name of the CSS file to be associated with the XML document (css.css). In the absence of the formatting file, the Web browser will act as a syntax parser and display the tree structure inherent in the XML document*

In the same way as for HTML documents, CSS instructions use specific syntax to determine the properties (font, size, spacing, borders, alignments, colors, position, etc.), which will be adapted on the basis of the documents themselves and the associated tags. Thus, a single style sheet can be shared by multiple documents (but conversely, an XML document may also obey multiple style sheets).

The ease with which "material formatting" and data documents can be combined opens up extremely rich possibilities for improving the presentation of Web pages. Thus, by generalizing the style sheets when designing a Website, it is possible to ensure overall visual consistency between all of the pages, much like what text-processing tools offer for printed documents. Besides the advantage of being able to quickly alter the graphical signature of a site, it is particularly wise to externalize the styling characteristics when the data are to be distributed to a variety of machines in different use contexts. Thus, the same content, stored in an XML document, can then be distributed specifically to a laser printer, a high-resolution computer screen, an high-definition television (HD TV), the screen of a mobile telephone or that of a personal digital assistant (PDA), taking account of the actual possibilities for the device in question to display that content.

One considerable advantage with CSS is that it applies identically to XML documents and HTML pages. The use of style sheets on these two types of structured documents enables all Website designers to gradually integrate the approach of rationalization, not only in the presentation of documents but also in the overall organization of the documentary objects making up the site.

## 3.6. Data visualization: shapes, CANVAS and SVG

XML's syntax is purely textual, as is that of HTML, but this does not mean their applicability is restricted to textual documents. On the contrary, in fact, very soon after the publication of the XML standard, tagging languages built upon XML emerged, which were and are appropriate for various specific domains such as mathematical notations (MathML), multimedia (SMIL), voice (VoiceXML), telephony (WML), etc.

For a long time, graphics processing in browsers remained very rudimentary, limited to the display of fixed or animated images. Interactivity with images was also not highly developed, concentrated mainly on the notion of their being an embed point for hyperlinks (with the possibility of defining different interactive areas within the same image). In spite of the W3 recommendations on Synchronized Multimedia Integration Language (SMIL) intended to fill that gap, the implementation and dissemination of SMIL in browsers has not been properly executed. It was the proprietary solution Flash, developed by US giant Apple, which became the standard in terms of creation and manipulation of vector graphics. Today, advertising banners and online games make intensive use of Flash, in spite of the need to install a dedicated plugin for each browser. Dynamic HTML[23] (DHTML), which combines JavaScript, Document Object Model (DOM) and CSS, and is supposed to serve the needs of Web designers to create interactive sites, has never managed to supplant Flash, notably because of operating difficulties, not just from one browser to another, but also from one version of the same browser to another.

In view of the increasingly-important role played by interactivity built into graphical objects, version 5 of HTML as released by the W3 included graphical functions supported by "HTML Canvas 2D Context"[24], SVG and CSS2-3.

With these new graphical functions integrated into the recent versions of the browsers, the members of the W3 offer a technological solution for information mining. The data Web, the interoperability mechanisms and, more recently, the phenomenon of Open Data and Linked Data feed into an infinite tangle of interwoven data which can only be appreciated in the form of a visual overview. The Open Source environment GEPHI[25] on its own represents a good example of the issues involved in data visualization (academic research and data journalism) which, as stated by M. Hascoët, aims to exploit the characteristics of global perception to facilitate certain tasks linked to information mining [HAS 04]:

– quick exploration of unknown collections of information;

– demonstration of relations between pieces of information and structures;

---

23 http://www.w3.org/Style/#dynamic.
24 http://www.w3.org/TR/2dcontext/, draft recommendation.
25 https://gephi.github.io/.

– finding of access paths for pertinent information;

– classified organization of the data.

"The purpose of visualization is cognitive amplification in terms of acquisition and use of information (lessening efforts in finding information, using visual representations to increase shape detection, allowing the combination of ideas, and using comprehension-support mechanisms)" [AUB 03, p. 3].

The possibilities for native graphic processing in HTML5 are based on three mechanisms:

– the element <canvas></canvas>, which calls bitmap graphical functions, predefined in JavaScript, on the fly (see Figure 3.8);

– the element <svg></svg>, which facilitates calling on the fly (Figure 3.9);

– shapes exploiting the peculiarities of CSS (Figure 3.10).

In the following examples, all three mechanisms are used to produce elementary geometric objects (circles, triangles, parallelograms, etc.), which are accompanied by textual elements.

Another important language for composite documents is SVG[26]. This is an XML language which facilitates the description of two-dimensional vector graphical sequences. It provides all the properties of the best graphic languages, and combines them with the advantages of maneuverability offered by XML. SVG is capable of displaying a very high-quality graphic at variable scales depending on the terminal on which it is executed (Figure 3.10).

Mechanisms of animation and interactivity (mouse events) can also be attached to every defined object. With HTML5, SVG sequences are built into the functions of the browsers and no longer require the installation of plugins, as is the case with Flash or PDF, for example. In addition, the creation of SVG sequences is facilitated by WYSIWYG graphical applications in export form (Adobe Illustrator™, GIMP, OpenOffice Draw, etc.).

---

26 http://www.w3.org/Graphics/SVG/About.

```
<html><body>
<canvas id="cvs" width="180"
height="150"style="border:1px solid
#c3c3c3;"></canvas>
<script>
var canvas =
document.getElementById("cvs");
varctx = canvas.getContext("2d");
ctx.fillStyle = "#000000";


/* triangle */
ctx.beginPath();
ctx.moveTo(100,110);
ctx.lineTo(150,10);
ctx.lineTo(150,110);
ctx.closePath();
ctx.fill();
* circle */
ctx.beginPath();
ctx.arc(50,75,30,0,2*Math.PI);
ctx.stroke();
* libelle */
ctx.font="20px Arial";
ctx.fillText("Circle",20,40);
ctx.fillText("Triangle",95,130);
</script>

</body></html>
```

**Figure 3.8.** *Two-dimensional canvas in HTML5. Between the opening and closing tags <canvas></canvas>, whose attributes (width and height) indicate the display area, the graphical objects are generated using predefined JavaScript methods (colors, styles, shading, transformations, etc.). While multiple Canvas sequences may be present in the same HTML5 document, the graphical objects produced on the fly rapidly by JavaScript can no longer be addressed individually (interaction with each element proves impossible), unlike with the possibilities afforded by SVG and CSS shapes*

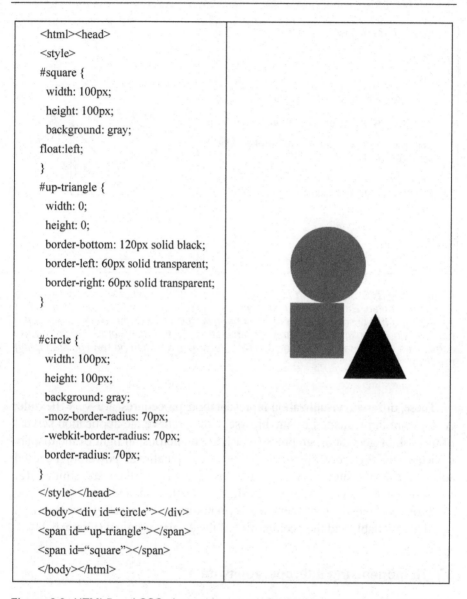

```
<html><head>
<style>
#square {
  width: 100px;
  height: 100px;
  background: gray;
float:left;
}
#up-triangle {
  width: 0;
  height: 0;
  border-bottom: 120px solid black;
  border-left: 60px solid transparent;
  border-right: 60px solid transparent;
}

#circle {
  width: 100px;
  height: 100px;
  background: gray;
  -moz-border-radius: 70px;
  -webkit-border-radius: 70px;
  border-radius: 70px;
}
</style></head>
<body><div id="circle"></div>
<span id="up-triangle"></span>
<span id="square"></span>
</body></html>
```

**Figure 3.9.** *HTML5 and CSS shapes document. Sophisticated geometric shapes are shaped from the CSS properties declared in the document header. The objects which are to be geometrically transformed appear very simply in the document body, owing to the <div></div> tags. They are then associated with the styles by identifiers or CSS classes*

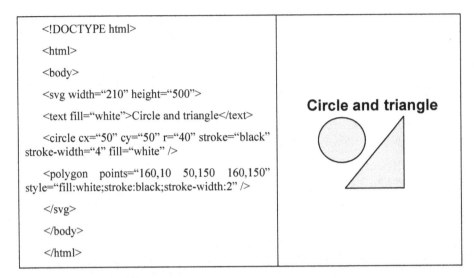

**Figure 3.10.** *SVG elements in an HTML5 document. Here, the tree structure of the XML is respected. Each included element can still be addressed and can be modified by adjusting the associated properties (changing the color of the circle, altering the size of the triangle, adding graphic animation to the text, etc). Multiple SVG sequences may appear in the same HTML document and can be manipulated using the DOM*

These different visualization/representation procedures are very flexible. As they are implemented by the browsers, they relieve the application servers of the task of generating graphics (which are numerous, in light of the display devices) and therefore allow the servers' computational power to be used solely for processing data. The processed data are then transmitted (in javascript object notation (JSON), XML or comma-separated values (CSV)) to the browsers, which implement the formatting on the basis of the technical solutions available and the peculiarities of the display terminal (Figure 3.11).

## 3.7. Homogenizing interoperability data

The creation of the structure of formatting objects is obtained by a transformation of the initial XML document into that formatting structure. The language XSL Transformation (XSLT) takes care of these transformations. Written in XML, XSLT appears as a high-level, non-procedural declarative language which offers the programmer control structures and numerous integrated functions (Table 3.2).

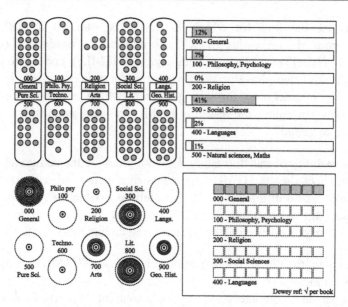

**Figure 3.11.** *Graphical objects produced on the fly in the browser on the basis of the Visual Catalog (http://www.titralog.com). The different elements use Canvas, SVG and CSS and are interactive. The four representations show the results of a document search in the bibliographical catalog of a library*

```
<?xml version="1.0" encoding="UTF-8"?>
<xsl:stylesheet version="2.0" xmlns:xsl="http://www.w3.org/1999/XSL/Transform">
<xsl:output method="xml" doctype-system="" doctype-public=""/>
<xsl:template match="/">
<html xmlns="http://www.w3.org/1999/xhtml">
<body>
<section>
<article>
<header><xsl:value-of select="page/title"/></header>
<main><xsl:value-of select="page/paragraph"/></main>
</article>
</section>
</body>
</html>
</xsl:template>
</xsl:stylesheet>
```

**Table 3.2.** *Formatting an HTML page with an XSLT script*

Surpassing the uses for which its designers intended it, XSLT soon deviated from its principles of XSL formatting to produce HTML (or eXtensible HyperText Markup Language (XHTML)) codes from XML documents. The two-phase process with transformation of XSL is similar, but instead of generating formatting objects which are specifically XSL (XSL-FO, in particular), the resulting HTML language is considered to be a formatting language.

This possibility of transformation does not preclude the additional use of a CSS style sheet on the HTML documents thus generated to improve their presentation. These different formatting solutions – which may at first glance seem redundant – constitute a set of tools that can be used to reconcile evolutivity and precedence of (fairly) structured documents from the Web.

There again, the visual reorganizations of XML or XHTML documents can be processed locally, on the fly, by the Internaut's browser. The computational power of personal computers and the sophistication of recent Web browsers enable us to deport processing which has, in the past, been done on the servers, to the users' own machines. It is the interoperability conditions which determine how the XSL transformations are handled: either by the Internaut's browser or by application servers authorized to exchange data.

Yet, until the recent past, the presence of a wide variety of versions of browsers, which worked differently from one operating system to another (notably because of the internal configurations), led developers to exercise prudence, by keeping on the servers various processing operations which could, technically, be transferred to the browsers. Also, the generalization of the Web browser on numerous lightweight terminals (such as cellphones, PDAs, tablets, games consoles, etc.), where certain resources were not available (video, animations, high-resolution images, etc.), slowed this tendency toward "downsizing" of software to prevent the needless transfer of data.

This situation is amplified by the possibilities of interoperability afforded by the plasticity of XML documents and applications. Indeed, the creation of a composite XML document, created because of a specific request from a remote user, can implement numerous other structured documents and multiple interconnected databases.

Software architectures which, themselves, are composite are used to design, on the fly, a new document crafted to respond to a request and designed for a specific type of terminal. This production of structured documents (XML, HTML and XHTML), from different sources, is not incompatible with the production of specific formats working in the browsers due to dedicated plugins (or *players*). This strategy is less and less used for the file format Shockwave Flash[27], developed by Macromedia (Adobe since 2005), but is still very frequently employed for PDF[28] from Adobe.

A composite document (constructed from fragments managed by different computer systems), considered to be a discrete object at the time of viewing, may have a variety of representations, depending on the visualization support used. Online newspapers, which use multimedia to enrich their articles, at the same time, offer the possibility of printing the articles in an appropriate PDF format. These printer-friendly versions are often free (or at least more free) of advertising banners and all the multimedia additions, and have a page header and footer which are not present in the online version of the article.

## 3.8. XML and DTD: *lingua franca* of technological interoperability

With XML, a veritable change has begun to take place on the Web of data structuring. Inspired by SGML, as HTML is, XML places emphasis on the issues of data exchange and interoperability, with the immediate questions of visualization (publication) of information being relegated to a secondary status. The mutation from a static Web to a dynamic Web, where the contents of the pages are no longer coded in distinct and addressable computerized entities (ASCII files) but instead in databases, has expedited the need to separate data from their display characteristics.

---

27 Since 1998, the specifications of Shockwave Flash executable files (.swf) have been publically available. They can be downloaded from Adobe's Website at http://www.adobe.com/devnet/swf/. Since that date, based on these specifications, software libraries written in C++, PHP, Python, Ruby and Perl have been made available by the Open Source development communities (http://sourceforge.net/projects/ming, http://www. libming.org/). These libraries can be used to dynamically create .swf executables outside of Adobe's development environments (Flash MX). The .swf files thus produced are perfectly compatible with the different players built into Web browsers.

28 PDF format is standardized by the ISO by ISO 32000-1:2008. PDF is an open format whose specifications are public and freely usable by any and all: (http://www.adobe.com/ devnet/pdf/).

The semantics of HTML tags, originally designed to serve the needs of dissemination of technical information to an audience of experts, well used to the peculiarities of scientific academic communication, has shifted to an audience who are less technically able and less sensitive to the appropriate use of formatting tags. Finally, the need to separate the fundament from the form has become greater with the mutation from the documentary Web toward the data Web.

XML is a meta-language which offers the possibility of freely producing original document formats while ensuring optimal integration of those documents into the Web (Table 3.3). The flexibility of XML is revealed by the limitless creative capacity of new tagging languages, which are able to adapt well to more complex or more specialized documents.

```
<?xml version="1.0" encoding="utf-8"?>
<resource>
<long_title>
<title />
<subtitle />
</long_title>
<authors>
<author />
</authors>
<publisher />
<collection />
<publisher />
<covers>
<title page />
<back cover>
<biographies>
<bio_author />
</biographies>
<description />
</back cover>
</covers>
<summary />
<keywords>
<keyword />
</keywords>
</resource>
```

**Table 3.3.** *The instance of an XML document (without raw data associated) in accordance with the previous DTD "work". The instance is said to be "well formed"*

Such is the case of digital libraries which offer descriptions of a wide variety of their digital resources. For example, the interoperability between the portal of the *Archives Audiovisuelles de la Recherche* (AAR, Audiovisual Research Archives – http://www.archivesaudiovisuelles.fr) and that of the *Université Ouverte des Humanités* (UOH, Open University of the Humanities – http://www.uoh.fr) is real, because some of the resources produced and described specifically in the AAR are present in the UOH portal. As the XML data models between the two environments are not identical, equivalences are established between the grammar for description of the documents in the AAR and that used by the UOH (Tables 3.4 and 3.5).

```
<lom:lomxmlns:lom="http://ltsc.ieee.org/xsd/LOM"
xmlns:lomfr="http://www.lom-fr.fr/xsd/LOMFR"
xmlns:xsi="http://www.w3.org/2001/XMLSchema-instance"
xsi:schemaLocation="http://ltsc.ieee.org/xsd/LOM http://lom-fr.fr/xsd/
lomfrv1.0/std/lomfr.xsd">

<lom:general>

<lom:identifier>

<lom:catalog>URI</lom:catalog>

<lom:entry>5d6c1d6a-121b-4eda-a8c4-ffbf39babf62</lom:entry>

</lom:identifier>

<lom:title>

<lom:string language="en">

Science: between knowledge and uncertainty (Course:Psychometry and
Statistics)

</lom:string>

</lom:title>

<lom:language>en</lom:language>

<lom:description>

<lom:string language="en">

Aims to show how Statistics has come to play its part in the field of
science. Indeed, with the development of empirical sciences, science's
perspective has shifted, from one where knowledge was made up of
absolute certainties based solely on the use of reason to one where the
uncertainty inherent in the material world is accepted.

</lom:string>

</lom:description>

<lom:keyword>

<lom:string language="en">empirical sciences</lom:string>
```

```
</lom:keyword>
<lom:keyword>
<lom:string language="en">certainty</lom:string>
</lom:keyword>
<lom:keyword>
<lom:string language="en">uncertainty</lom:string>
</lom:keyword>
<lom:keyword>
<lom:string language="en">partial ignorance</lom:string>
</lom:keyword>
...
```

**Table 3.4.** *A partial XML instance (in LOM-fr format) from the digital portal of the UOH (http://www.uoh.fr)*

```
<?xml version="1.0" encoding="utf-8"?>
<Sheetxmlns:xsd="http://www.w3.org/2001/XMLSchema"
xmlns:xsi="http://www.w3.org/2001/XMLSchema-instance">
<Identifier>99_413_1162</Identifier>
<id_parent>99</id_parent>
<title>Folkloric tradition in popular culture – interview – The wooden horse
dance</title>
<url>http://www.archivesaudiovisuelles.fr/99</url>
<urlplayer>http://www.archivesaudiovisuelles.fr/FR/_video.asp?id=99&res
s=413&video=90841&format=69</urlplayer>
<distinction />
<description>
&lt;b&gt;Jean-Claude SCHMITT&lt;/b&gt; is the Director of Studies at
EHESS (Ecole des Hautes Etudes en Sciences Sociales – Social Sciences
Higher Education Institute) and head of GAHOM (Groupe d'Anthropologie
Historique de l'Occident Médieval – Medieval Occidental Historical
Anthropology Group).
</description>
<contacts>
...
```

**Table 3.5.** *Partial XML instance from a resource at France's Archives Audiovisuelles de la Recherche (http://www.archivesaudiovisuelles.fr)*

The establishment of equivalence, in the context of interoperability between documentary platforms, cannot be based solely on the instances of XML documents. The conditions of repetition of the elements or types of data expected, for instance, are not rigorously transmitted by the instances. In Table 3.5, as the tag <description> is empty, there is no way of knowing whether it contains subelements. Document Type Definitions (DTDs) and XML Schemas are grammar description languages, used to describe all the constraints and conditions of realization of the instances as a function of the available data (see Table 3.6).

```
<?xml version="1.0" encoding="ISO-8859-1" ?>

<!ELEMENT resource (long_title+, authors+, publisher+, collection?, covers?, summary, keywords)>

<!ELEMENT long_title (title, subtitle?)>

<!ELEMENT title (#PCDATA)>

<!ELEMENT subtitle (#PCDATA)>

<!ELEMENT authors (author)+>

<!ELEMENT author (#PCDATA)>

<!ELEMENT collection (#PCDATA)>

<!ELEMENT publisher (#PCDATA)>

<!ELEMENT summary (#PCDATA)>

<!ELEMENT keywords (keyword)*>

<!ELEMENT keyword (#PCDATA)>

<!ELEMENT covers (titlepage, back cover)>

<!ELEMENT title page (#PCDATA)>

<!ELEMENT back cover (biographies, description)>

<!ELEMENT biographies (bio_author)+>

<!ELEMENT description (#PCDATA)>

<!ELEMENT bio_author (#PCDATA)>
```

**Table 3.6.** *The XML DTD of a publication. This explicit illustration of the logical structure represents the generic logical model common to all the variations of this type of document (publication). The usefulness of a DTD becomes apparent when we consider that all the possible variations (instances) will conform to the model. Parsers are software tools which can check the validity of an instance against a referential model*

The DTD from Table 3.6 here expressing a publication (<resource>, root element), generic entity, is characterized by various sub-elements (<long_title>, <authors>, <collection>, <covers>, etc.) which, themselves, may potentially be made up of subelements (the note #PCDATA indicates that the element is terminal). The characters "?" (question mark), * (asterisk) and + (plus) assume a particular significance in DTDs [MIC 98, HEW 90]. They follow the names of the elements and indicate their presence and the number of repetitions:

– question mark (?): the element must appear either once only or not at all;

– asterisk (*): the element may appear multiple times;

– plus (+): the element must appear at least once.

DTDs improve the quality of XML instances, because they (the latter) are validated before their use. They also enable us to envisage unforeseen equivalences between instances extracted from different sources (for which DTDs are known) and an output format designed to serve particular needs.

As it is possible to process the instances of XML documents (and their DTD) independently of any linguistic specialization, the use of meaningful lexical expressions drawn from any given natural language to construct the label of the tags is ultimately not recommended – particularly as XML documents are not intended to be read, but simply processed [MIC 98]. In addition, this tendency to use lexical expressions that are meaningful for a human operator for the tags complexifies the documents with *namespaces* to make the common tags arising from distinct classes of documents less ambiguous (particularly during XSLT processing applied to multiple XML documents).

These treatments are determined by the DOM[29] which defines the logical structure of XML (or HTML) documents and the mechanisms to access and manipulate them. Due to DOM specifications, developers can use an Application Programming Interface (API) to construct documents, explore their structure, add, modify and delete tags and content in an XML document.

While DTD is a powerful tool to validate the consistency of the data, it is not able to guarantee the effective content of the tags, as do (e.g.) the

---

29 http://www.w3.org/TR/1998/REC-DOM-Level-1-19981001/.

mechanisms of constraints of integrity of relational database management systems. XML Schema Definitions[30] (XSDs) improve DTDs by controlling the types of data and authorizing the namespaces (Table 3.7).

```
<?xml version="1.0"?>
<xs:schemaxmlns:xs="http://www.w3.org/2001/XMLSchema"
targetNamespace="http://www.site.com"
xmlns="http://www.site.com" elementFormDefault="qualified">

<xs:element name="mail">
<xs:complexType>
<xs:sequence>
        <xs:element name="priority" type="xs:string"/>
        <xs:element name="sender" type="xs:string"/>
        <xs:element name="addressee" type="xs:string"/>
        <xs:element name="ccs" type="xs:string"/>
        <xs:element name="ccs" maxOccurs="unbounded">
        <xs:complexType>
                <xs:element name="cc" type="xs:string"/>
        </xs:complexType>
        <xs:element name="bccs" maxOccurs="unbounded">
        <xs:complexType>
                <xs:element name="bcc" type="xs:string"/>
        </xs:complexType>
        <xs:element name="object" type="xs:string"/>
        <xs:element name="body" type="xs:string"/>
        <xs:element name="attachments" maxOccurs="unbounded">
        <xs:complexType>
        <xs:sequence>
                <xs:element name="attachment" type="xs:hexBinary"/>
        </xs:sequence>
        </xs:complexType>
</xs:sequence>
</xs:complexType>
</xs:element>
</xs:schema>
```

**Table 3.7.** *An XML schema to validate the instances of an XML document ("mail")*

---

30 http://www.w3.org/XML/Schema.

This form of organization, with a distinction being drawn between data, models (DTDs and schemas), processing (XSLT and XSF-FO), personalized virtual documents and the final document (XML+CSS, HTML and XHTML), ensures optimal construction of an object designed for the technical characteristics of a given viewing/printing peripheral device.

Due to the rigor that schemas bring to the structure, the processes become more secure. When an application works on a document which respects a known schema, it prevents unforeseen situations, and consequently unexpected results. This conceptual architecture renders the interoperability of data management systems (in the broadest sense) particularly productive and the logical/physical independence (data/processing) which enables us to adapt to any new support and multiple usage conditions.

## 3.9. Plasticity of content and dissolution of documents

In view of the diversity of the viewing devices, the flexibility of the interoperability of Web applications borne by XML technologies and the generalization of the dynamic Web, the possibilities of adapting the final form of an XML document, building it or transforming it are, essentially, limitless. "Personalized Virtual Documents" (PVDs) [AMG 08, CHA 06a, BOU 04, PAP 03a, GAR 99], which are largely composed of all kinds of fragments, extracted from different information systems, possibly hosted on distant machines, have no predefined size or form (see Figure 3.12)[31].

The possible forms of personalized virtual documents (PVD), and the information (data and metadata) contained therein, constitute only a circumstantial, ephemeral state, depending directly on the physical characteristics of the display devices, in conjunction with the user's demands. At a given moment in time, on the last peripheral device for which it has been created, on the basis of the fragments having contributed to its design, the final document is homogenized in a particular format (HTML, XHTML, PDF, SVG, XML, etc.).

---

31 A blog article is a sophisticated but commonplace example of a personalized virtual document. Indeed, aside from the textual and graphical elements, the article may be linked to external data (integrated videos, RSS feeds, AJAX scripts, etc.) and comments.

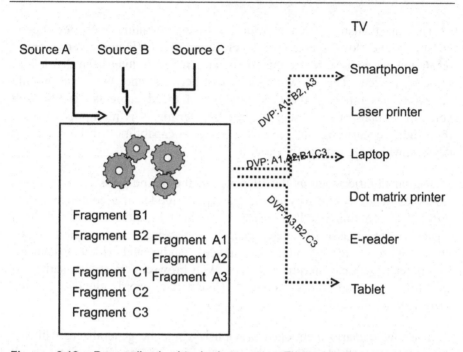

**Figure 3.12.** *Personalized virtual documents. These digital documents are ephemeral and only exist on the basis of the features of the reading device. No a priori form is associated with the collected data, which form a collection that makes sense for the Internaut. This syndicative object no longer has the status of a document, but a hypertext network extended by different reading paths. This object is still evolutive and constitutes an entirely separate resource in its own right. Digital libraries lend themselves to the extraction of such fragments: a video resource extracted from an AV resource portal can be integrated into a resource with articles from different review portals and bibliographical elements extracted from online catalogs*

Upstream, various scenarios of design of the final form of those PVDs may be envisaged. They depend, first, on the information systems managing the data necessary for the building of the document, and second, on the complexity of the document and the possible representations. Typically, middleware applications (PHP Hypertext Processor (PHP), Active Server Page (ASP), Java Server Page (JSP), etc.) [SAL 99] take care of the interrogation of the additional applications from which the data fragments are extracted. These middleware programs take care of the repatriation of the data, implement the collection from distinct data sources and finally format the final document in accordance with the user's expectations and the viewing/printing device used.

This mechanism, which is widely used by dynamic Web developers, constitutes the "low" scenario of development of a PVD in the very specific technological context where the computer screen has long been the default viewing device. The growing closeness between the Web and mobile telephony has rendered the dissemination of the documents via the Web complex, because the number of receiving terminals is multiplied. Today, the "high" scenarios are linked to the technical capabilities of the rendering devices, which are extremely variable.

Digital libraries such as the Websites of the online press are significant examples of the complexity of the conceptual model of a complete virtual document containing all possible personalized settings. The diffused contents are massively heterogeneous, because they exploit texts, photographs, static and animated images, audio and video sequences. Computer programs interpreted by the Web browser (client-side scripting) are fully part of those contents (interactive word clouds, graphic visualization of the elements of the document, etc.).

The low scenario mentioned previously could be generalized, with the option to respond algorithmically (in the form of specific scripts) to all new viewing supports. This approach, in the current context of diversification of connected terminal devices, seems unsatisfactory, because it leads to a proliferation of dedicated microapplications. Its main drawback lies in the heavy dependence of the data on the processing and the significant consequences in terms of evolutivity and subsequent software maintenance.

In this context, (documentary) Web technologies reduce the maintenance costs (by limiting application developments), preserve the independence of data and processing, and quickly adapt to the diversity of peripheral viewing devices due to ranges of presentation using XSLT transformation mechanisms.

High scenarios using XML technologies (formats and tools), on the other hand, require fuller modeling of the generic documentary structure, giving rise to specific documentary realizations. The generic documentary model feeds into an overall DTD which becomes the conceptual reference for the production of the documentary objects appropriate for the specialized output devices. This DTD ensures the consistency of the elements by explicitly stating the order, composition and hierarchy of the tags. The obligatory or optional nature of certain elements and the fact of their being unique or repeatable are a few of the indications enabling us to control the documentary instances produced.

Owing to standardization (W3 and ISO) and to the computer tools respecting the defined recommendations (client software, application servers and application libraries), the open formats of structured documents have reached the stage of maturity, and deliver maximum interoperability of the documents produced and modified. Today, the operative perennity of the documents is preserved by the fact that those standardized document formats are independent of the computer applications. Indeed, the flexibility of XML-based languages and the power of a DOM, widely distributed in the communities of developers, ensure the evolutivity of the document structures without breaking with the requirement of legibility and (re)processing of the documents created previously.

## 3.10. Interoperability for use: a looped technological loop

In view of the advent of the social and participative Web marked by human activities and community-based information mining, the data Web has supplanted the documentary Web, with a crucial role once again being played by automated data production and machine processing, as only machines are capable of reconstructing the semantics in the profusion of all sorts of digital data.

In keeping with the pragmatic directives of the World Wide Web Consortium, the most influential technological and economic members on the planet have, in the space of a few years, resolved the technological puzzle of production, processing and dissemination of digital information. The communications protocols, data formats and software platforms have lent operational consistency to those directives, which these influential members have not only promoted in their productions but also integrated into their way of working.

By their strategic collaboration, these major economic actors have gradually steered away from the initial goal of the dissemination and sharing of knowledge, as conceived by Tim Berners-Lee. Without abandoning the humanistic essence of that project, work has become more orientated toward economic and profitable ways of thinking. With unprecedented financial resources at their disposal, and due to technologies which they have helped to define, these multinationals have contributed to the validation of the effectiveness and performance of a broad range of W3 productions. Worldwide digital architectures have been constructed, wherein technological interoperability was essential for the purposes of communication and data exchanges between interconnected, modular, evolutive and distributed computer systems.

Digital libraries, which were set up by government initiatives, have inherited conceptual and technological productions from the largest enterprises in the world in terms of computing, software engineering and electronics. Such libraries have also benefited from those companies' cumulative experience in the implementation of these powerful and robust architectures. These technological models are too heavily marked by the issues of competing businesses. They have overshadowed the techno-documentary architectures for scientific, institutional, cultural, heritage (etc.) purposes, designed to provide quality free-to-access digital resources to a wide audience. The latter have remained based on technological data exchange logics which are incapable of adequately serving the needs of civilian users/Internauts or the goals of the public digital programs.

Nonetheless, digital technologies have reached an unprecedented level of maturity. The uncomplicated mechanisms of processing well-structured data, exploited confidentially by sophisticated computing platforms until fairly recently, have now been entrusted to the users themselves, being handled on the native machine by the Web browser – a universal application for the communication, processing and visualization of information. The power of personal computers and the speed of circulation of digital information in high-capacity domestic networks (e.g. digital subscriber line (DSL) and fiber-optic) mean that any Internaut can reconfigure data and information gleaned from all over the Web and from quality digital collections, to suit his/her activities.

The digital libraries financed by governmental projects to help citizens keep up with the transformation of today's society into the "Information Society" are – because of the technological paradigm of interoperability which they have integrated and from which they are unable to move on – incapable of serving this goal in ways which safeguard the acceptability and usability of the technical devices.

However, user-oriented interoperability, taking account of the vast range of uses, can be envisaged without major technological redefinition. The feasibility of this new interoperability is illustrated by the multinational giants such as Amazon, Facebook, Microsoft, etc., by the digital services they implement using API.

The free digital services of Amazon Web Services offer a good example of these mechanisms, which any digital library should now be able to provide to any user. Specifically, they employ the software architectural style "REST" (Representational State Transfer), which uses HTTP to transmit numerous requests aimed at finding a particular resource (Itemsearch), exploring the collections or a subset of those collections (BrowseNodeLookup), or discovering resources similar to those which the user has selected (SimilarityLookup).

For example, an ItemSearchRequest to find all books dealing with "sustainable development" would be expressed as follows:

http://webservices.amazon.com/onca/xml?Service=AWSECommerceSer vice&Version=2015-08-01&Operation=ItemSearch&SearchIndex=Books &Keywords=sustainable+development

– The ParameterSearchIndex indicates the category of resources sought, and can take one of a number of predetermined values, including, most notably, the following: books, DVD, music, apparel, video, jewelry, automotive, watches, electronics, etc.

– The parameter keywords reproduces the terms of the user's search in coded form.

To these three requests, which may be transmitted directly by the Web browser or by a script (PHP, JavaScript, activer server pag (ASP), etc.), the Amazon platform responds with an XML document which is generally used in interapplicational technological interoperability.

The Web portals of topical digital universities, online catalogs, review portals, the resources of the *Institut National De l'Audiovisuel* (INA), universities' digital collections, etc., can integrate this vocabulary of interrogation and data extraction into their architecture, with no particular technological difficulty. Otherwise, the OAI-PMH harvesting services which they employ – another resurgence of a system-oriented design and similar style of technological interoperability – are more difficult to implement.

Finally, technological interoperability as envisaged between digital libraries considerably impoverishes the descriptions of each of those libraries; notably, there is no need for equivalence and alignment of the tags. If – as happens with the available digital resources – the descriptions (DTDs) of the resources and their forms of organization (collections, categories, themes, classifications, etc.) were disseminated together, digital libraries would manifest an evolution toward the user paradigm (and its uses). In this case, Internauts would once again be given control of their selections and the hybrid recompositions of content that constitute the major advantage to these new techno-documentary architectures.

# 4

## Usage Prospects

### 4.1. Technological, semantic and cultural interoperability

The freedom of all European citizens to work and live anywhere in the European Union has necessitated unprecedented procedures of cooperation between the Member States in order to make that legal liberty into a *de facto* freedom. Below the surface of this major evolution, what European citizens expect is a significant modernization of administration and administrative practices. From this new political and economic configuration, the Europeans demand a reduction in administrative isolationism and genuine quality of service in terms of access and individualized treatment [ASS 07, FLI 04, SAU 02].

This cooperation has resulted in the establishment of shared information flows between the information systems of the European public administration bodies. Technological interoperability has proved an absolute necessity in order for hitherto-independent information architectures to work together without compromising the autonomy, sovereignty and security of each state of the European Union (see Figure 4.1).

The interoperability to which European states adhere today is presented as "the ability of disparate and diverse organizations to interact in order to achieve mutually-advantageous common goals, governed by mutual agreement, involving the sharing of information and knowledge between those organizations through the professional processes that they undertake, by the exchange of data between their respective Information and Communication Systems (ICT) systems".

The extremely important role played by ICT in this process of interoperability confirms the maturity of the technological propositions and, more specifically, the standards and recommendations that the W3 and its international industrialist members have been producing and implementing since the creation of the Consortium: "Recentering the use of the standards used on critical issues of interoperability at the 'boundaries' and beyond the boundary of the of each ministry, administration, operator, collective, etc. (…) An interoperability profile contains a set of standards and recommendations about specific use cases" [DIR 15, p. 4].

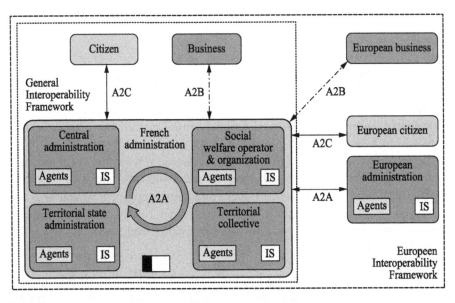

**Figure 4.1.** *The Référentiel Général d'Interopérabilité (General Interoperability Framework) – focuses on France's administration. The figure distinguishes between the different types of exchanges between the actors (the administration – A2A; the citizen – A2C and business – A2B).This principle is transferrable to each of the Member States of the European Union. The A2A relation represents the exchange of information that each country can undertake with all the others, and the exchanges which each of them can have with the administrative authorities of the European Union (the Commission, the Parliament, the Central European Bank, etc.)*

Although improving services to users – European citizens – constitutes an essential element in the phenomenal digital field at hand, the efficiency, quality, acceptability and usability of these new devices and the inherent procedures can only be measured after a true evaluation. The technological solutions adopted are ultimately identical to those adopted not only by the major economic actors but also, to a lesser extent in terms of sociotechnical impacts, the designers of digital libraries. These measures generalize and render the artifactualization of our societies, which are becoming digital, commonplace [PAP 14a, TGE 11, BER 08, JOC 08].

By subscribing to Web technologies, administrations and businesses of all sizes can benefit from high-performing computer solutions, that are simple to install and easy to use. By adopting them, they are assured of inheriting an optimal mechanism of organization and management of informational processes, similar to larger enterprises which have generalized the use of Web technologies in their Intranets, for reasons of efficiency: "The protocol IP and its main incarnation, the Web, facilitate the establishment of applications at a reduced cost, make administrative tasks easier, and render distances insignificant. These are all assets for SMEs, which now have at their disposal an information system providing services which have hitherto been the preserve of very large enterprises."

Introduced in the home, in business and in public administration, ICT imposes its regulating and amplifying omnipresence on everybody. The growing role played by the "digital economy" and the normalization of human communications mediated by ICT are indicative of the extent of this omnipresence [BIG 12, MAT 05, RIF 05, THE 02]. For more than a decade, the partisan political and technoscientific discourse has been tirelessly promoting decidedly digital economic directions, which are gages of growth and competitiveness in a climate of general globalized competition . Human activities – professional, collective, managerial, social, pleasurable, personal, informational, educational, etc. – are irrigated by intrusive digital technologies which trace a circular continuum from home to school, from home to university, or from home to work [DOU 08].

Amplified by technological normalization orchestrated by powerful economic, governmental and technological consortiums, the digital wave is homogenizing professional practices and emerging as a support/vector for phenomenal plasticity, capable of adapting to all the cognitive tasks of users engaged in processes of education or lifelong training [BER 08, MEY 09].

In parallel to this phenomenon, vast fields of scientific and technical knowledge, considered humanity's scientific and cultural heritage, are being placed online in textual and multimedia digital libraries financed by the states, in order to serve the expectations and needs of all Internauts who are *naturally* accustomed to the techniques of "information mining" [DIN 14, IHA 08, DIN 08, SIM 02]. The increasingly-heterogeneous documentary resources, disseminated across the Web, are based upon and infinitely reproduce standardized means of viewing and representing information (HyperText Markup Language (HTML), eXtensible HyperText Markup Language (XHTML) and Cascading StyleSheet (CSS)), reading mechanisms marked by hypertext associativity and browsing, and finally search procedures that are heavily influenced by the elementary logic of search engines and business directories.

However, as is pointed out by Pavé [PAV 89] and Wolton [WOL 00] – and illustrated by the difficulties in providing the *Très Grande Bibliothèque Nationale* (Very Large National Library) project with user technology that conforms to the expectations of all the different categories of prospective readers (computer-assisted reading for prolific readers) [SOU 01, MAN 00, MAN 99, STI 95, VIR 93] – computer technology cannot, alone, come up with an organizational system; it is not able to solve problems which human activity has not managed to solve; and invariably it is plagued by the complexity of vernacular implementation and use.

The issues relate to size, because the situation is a synecdoche of the way in which the "Information Society" works, in terms of construction and the technological and cognitive interfaces which need to be created so that the system is easy to use for as many people as possible. The increased economic and institutional power of that Information Society, the complexity of organization and operation that it involves and with which all the actors have to deal, require informational and technological skills and abilities of a similar level to those necessitated by the heterogeneity and diversity of the documentation now available from libraries.

These new skills will increasingly be required for the judicial construction of the information society governed by the digital economy and misdemeanors in terms of computer fraud, rumor propagation, defamation, illegal use of peer-to-peer systems, intellectual property, use of confidential data, privacy invasion, etc. The legal regulation of the Internet [CAL 07, AMB 05, MAT 05] now gives every Internaut certain rights and responsibilities.

## 4.2. Content and documents in digital libraries

Over the past two decades, the electronic document (which is a digital copy of an original paper document), managed by sophisticated and costly electronic document manager (EDM) devices, has been transformed to such a degree that now the document itself is only an individual expression of the content, which is governed by the formatting supports that users can employ differently or similarly. The technological approach taken by content management systems (CMSs) is indicative of the disappearance of a specific form of the document in favor of heterogeneous, proteiform and infinitely-combinable content. *De facto*, the usage conditions imposed by the multitude of client devices on which the content can be viewed necessitate very high plasticity of these digital data so that they can be tailored to suit technical viewing conditions, transport methods and usage. That is to say, the documents may assume a multitude of possible forms, because the angular building-blocks which facilitate this digital polymorphism are operational: storage formats, management systems and distribution systems, formalisms of reference, links and identification.

In the name of maximum interoperability of information systems – and consequently, the certainty of improving communication – the technique imposes a viewpoint which, today, is marked by "digital content". By separation of the container and its contents, of the substance and the form, ICT is the final step in a sophisticated process of dematerialization of information. The modularity, extensibility and openness which characterize digital content are designed to take account of all usage conditions. "The development of XML and of the associated technologies opens up new possibilities in the area of hypermedia. These technologies can be applied through the Web, and thus are available to a very large number of users. They also enable us to link highly-distributed informational resources. Represented using the XML model, these resources may be the subject of very varied treatments" [QUI 03, p. 123]. By opening up the "world of the possible" in terms of data processing, ICT extends the possibilities of use, which, by cyclical repercussion, also extends the possible usages.

The digital document is a technological document which is indissociable from the ICT that implements it. This document, which introduces combinatorial diversity of the content, redefines the relationship between content and usage. The form of the document – that presentation which cannot simply be reduced to the page setting or the formatting of the characters – carries with it a diverse set of semiotic usage values. Depending on the form the information takes (an article, report, note, working document, memorandum, book, etc.), a piece of information with the same content will also bear meta-information which gives the user an indication of the intellectual accessibility, the degree of specialty, the target or the degree of advancement of the project.

Besides the fact that the document is present in all knowledge capitalization approaches, it is linked to human lifecycles: it is born, grows and evolves and is employed in a time period which is that of the human context and social context. Thus, different processes enter into play, with these processes being organized over time by the individual or by the community: the design period (author and sources used) and the exploitation period (consultation and referencing). From the usage to the appropriation of the artifacts, the subjects' activity is a development where the dimensions of goal-fulfillment and realization of the tasks of productive activity hinge upon the dimensions of elaboration of external and internal resources of the constructive activity. Productive and constructive activities are inextricably linked to human activity. They mutually enrich and transform one another: a difficulty encountered with the productive aspect could necessitate the development of resources on the constructive level which, in return, modify the forms and conditions of the productive activities. More than ever, in spite of the present political and industrial climate, ICT must be used properly. It can only be used following observation and analysis of the users' informational needs when the intellectual and organizational environment and the users' objectives are known. The aim here is not to develop self-proclaimed technical logics which are founded on models of the user (the user paradigm), breaking with the realities of informational practices (novices and expert users), but instead to produce technical improvements, not forgetting that "…an individual's relevance system is a psychological state of predisposition questioning the cognitive, affective, perceptive and behavioral. It is on the basis of the set of specific problems which preoccupy the individual, the projects s/he has, that form his/her life orientation at the moment in question…" [MUC 01, p. 67].

## 4.3. Digital interfaces for the information society

In 1968, Douglas Engelbart, the American engineer and technological visionary, inventor of the mouse and pioneer of man–machine dialog, drawing inspiration from Bush's musings, created the NLS/Augment system – a sort of *avant-garde* collaborative hypertext system (coupled with a videoconferencing system) whose purpose was to show how technical orthesis would help to amplify humans' intellectual abilities. In 1975, Theodor Holm Nelson, the American philosopher, took up the principles of hypertext for his own purposes. It was Nelson who coined that term, and through the Utopian "Xanadu Project", hypertext came to represent all that is carried by the term "accessibility". With the Internet and *ad hoc* digital technologies reaching genuine technological maturity in the space of only 10 years, this desire for maximum access to a large amount of information has not only been more than delivered upon, but has also actually become completely integrated into humans' social, educational, cultural and professional (etc.) activities.

With hypertext use becoming widespread since the 1990s, the interface between man and information is reduced to its simplest form: a software artifact (the Web browser) which activates links between documents based on associations guided by the reader's choices. The individual is at the heart of all information searches, as the initiator and actor of the reading choices which construct personalized paths appropriate for the circumstances of his/her reading. Since the very earliest implementations (often supplied on Compact-Disc, Read Only Memory (CD-ROM)), this possibility of navigating through the ocean of information has had some worrying side-effects: readers of cross-linked hypertexts soon become afflicted by disorientation and cognitive overload. Although they are unavoidable, it was not until very late in the game that these effects were analyzed by cognitive sciences and psychology, which were ill-equipped to study them. The rise of the Web's power, rendering the most elementary principles of hypertext very easy to implement, has meant that hypertext documents are now produced and used all over the world. The digital world has become a reality[1].

The frantic pace of innovation in digital technologies (pervasive computing and digital roaming) feeds a proportional mutation of the uses made by an innumerable audience, whose shifting and overlapping profiles are impossible to grasp. The experimental protocols of psychology, befuddled by these changes of scale, have difficulty in establishing

---

1 A reality analyzed in France by researchers in a variety of academic disciplines, brought together to from the *Observatoire des Mondes Numériques en Sciences Humaines* (OMNSH).

sustainable and generalizable results in regard to the relationship, which is constantly renewed by technological mediation of the individual with informational resources. Although it has not produced any immediate solutions, scientific research on the recurrent issues of disorientation and cognitive overload when consulting sets of heavily linked documents has been able to identify composite elements and improve the understanding of the mechanisms of appearance. These results, however modest they may be, lead to an ambivalent re-examination of the emergence of the information society.

First, the worldwide rollout of the technological resources offered by ICT (derived from the Internet) is the vector of a democratization of our relationship with information in today's society. The easy and widespread production and dissemination of, and access to, all sorts of information – primarily digital – are becoming imposed as fundamental functions of the information society. The recent but powerful phenomenon of the social Web marks the "completion" of a sparked mutation: from the technological Web of its early days, which has shifted from a position of techno-scientific visibility to that of an underground, powerful and ubiquitous infrastructure to which all citizens are led to subscribe. The edification of the information society upon this permanent infrastructure redefines human activity in all its richness. The technological Web, which has developed on the basis of the spectacular progress made in recent years, has lent stability to tools, formats and protocols which have become standards. Today, this standardization provides us with a robust design framework, appropriate for innovative achievements in the domain of ICT. These innovations benefit from a worldwide field of propagation, due to the interoperability of digital technologies. The participative Web, built on the instrumental manifestations of these innovations, encompasses a vast range of human activities – individual, collective, professional, social, cultural, political, etc.

Second, the results of the experiments conducted over the past few years in specific contexts, often linked to educational environments (school, university, business, etc.), systematically indicate that the instrumental geneses which hold the key to the appropriation of the technical environments' techniques by users are particularly fragile. The constant modifications to the technical parameters of the information (and communication) systems, to some extent, have a negative effect on innovation, slowing down the complex process of instrumental genesis. The growing role of technical mediation – notably that involving the communications instrumented by ICT in professional environments, whatever the sectors of economic activity – exerts significant pressure on individuals. They must demonstrate their ability to make proper use of the new technologies, to perceive the possibilities and limitations of computer-based processing, to be critical of the results of that processing and identify the legal and social constraints on these uses. The widespread tools and Web services used in both the private and professional spheres considerably blur the lines by drawing on practices that overlap (information retrieval, messaging, downloading, etc.), but whose consequences may be damaging for the citizen, employee and/or company using them.

This observation tempers governmental enthusiasm based on the target figure of systematic rise in the amount of household computer equipment and its connection to the Internet. It highlights the fact that in terms of the use of ICT, envisaged in the context of the information society for all, the indispensable technological and informational skills cannot be derived from a little practice and self-training in the private and family context (much like *digital natives*). These skills must be constructed in accordance with the rigorous methodologies enabling the individual to appreciate the growth in his/her own skills, their true effectiveness and the refinement of their ability to mobilize proportionally to their use context. Thus, the question of the digital divide, hitherto dealt with in the considerations of material equipment (computing and telecommunications), has not been completely avoided with the falling cost of equipment, but instead has been doubled by considering the risks of social inequalities, cognitive divide, economic competition exacerbated by digital technology (economic intelligence) and the invasion of our private lives.

However, the systematic software-based mechanization of the information systems of private and public organizations is attended by a sort of evidence nourished by the designers in terms of technical manipulation which tends to influence inherent intellectual abilities. Ultimately, these information systems are only ingredients designed to enliven a lengthy process requiring transformation on the part of the individuals, understanding and self-awareness, awareness of others and the systems – whatever they may be – within which they are evolving, be it by choice or by lack thereof. In this design, independently of any technological consideration, the individual's capacity to apprehend – and ideally to appropriate – that information is far from being achieved. It is based on abilities, strategies and *savoir-faire* which everyone must adapt and draw upon over the course of the social, cultural and cognitive experiences which he/she will have in life.

Disinformation, information overload, information deficit..., etc. We could also express the secondary effects linked to information by noise, silence, (ir)relevance, etc., which go hand-in-hand with the very notion of information and are indicative of the difficulty in finding a sort of satisfactory homeostasis: the correct information to suit the right request, at the right time, in phase with the receiver's comprehension capabilities, whatever the technological conditions of emission, transmission and receipt of the information.

From a societal point of view, the situation becomes more complex. It becomes particularly complicated for the individual. On the other hand, though, with digital homogenization, the transformation of documents into digital content and digital streams becomes easier and is sped up.

In the space of 15 years, digital documentary environments designed to serve heritage, cultural, scientific or commercial requirements have become established in cyberspace throughout the world, and have redefined the techno-documentary landscape of the World Wide Web [AND 12, PAP 11, SCH 00]. However, while the technological models, which are heavily inspired by the work of the W3, have proved their (technological) effectiveness, and largely account for the creation of libraries, archives and digital depots, the underlying concept continues to fuel debate within the community of documentary actors, with emphasis being placed on the use of these digital documentary environments [VID 13, MOA 13, CHE 11b, DAV 07, CIA 05, BOR 04].

Digital libraries that are massively interoperable, from a technological point of view, now offer heterogeneous content (text, image, sound and video) which requires additional descriptions (indexing metadata, generic or specific metadata, etc.) in order to be truly usable for an audience with many different informational profiles. Although the computer technologies upon which heterogeneous digital libraries are built facilitate the technical interoperability of the content, they are not sufficient to guarantee the adhesion of an audience connected with highly-varying informational and technical profiles.

## 4.4. Information searching and interoperable technological architectures

The generalist search engines that Internauts have been using on a huge scale for the past two decades have encapsulated the practice of information-seeking in searching for lexical sequences (keywords, controlled expressions and complete text), which is now proving to be a major handicap in the process of value-creation/exploitation of audiovisual resources in particular [IHA 04]. For these resources, it is mainly the added descriptive data which determine the ability to find the digital documents (accessibility/availability) and to locate them within the existing scientific and technical collections [ROL 09, SOE 05].

However, value creation from academic audiovisual production is based on substandard indexing mechanisms which employ either the restrictive normalized cataloging procedures used by information professionals (librarians and archivists) or free indexing (folksonomies and communities of practice) [MAT 12, MOR 08]. This situation tends to confine that digital content in "digital depots" which are hard to find and are isolated in digital working environments [ZAC 10, KOO 05, BOU 03, SMI 03].

These two approaches to metadescription – the first specialized, and the second uncontrollable and unsatisfactory – thus limit the exploitation of resources by a wide audience [PIR 10, PAP 07b, ROY 03]. The use of a range of specialized descriptors (RAMEAU, MotBis, LCSH, etc.) renders searches difficult for any user who is unfamiliar with documentary languages. Conversely, the absence of rigor in the modes of indexing leads to user searches that are uncertain and random.

In all these documentary devices, however, the computing technologies employed (formats and tools) for the majority of Web technologies developed by the members of the W3, are intended for use in an encapsulating and syndicative approach to interoperability [BON 12]. These computer technologies, which are functionally Web-oriented, have been developed as interoperability technologies capable of adapting to specific operating conditions (portal, syndication platform, Virtual Private Network (VPN), etc.).

In addition, they are proprietary solutions such as open source solutions which are based on the W3C's Web technologies [PAP 11, BAC 09]. The multiple documentary portals and the numerous digital libraries which offer considerable volumes of all sorts of documents, whether to open access or not, are therefore governed by the same principles of construction, feeding and usage regardless of the computer systems used [TGE 11]. It is not uncommon to see these documentary systems boasting the ability to interface with other devices, in spite of having very different design processes. Such is the case with the journal portal in the area of social and human sciences, Persee.fr (free access), which states on its site : "Now, the academic community has easy access to complete collections of journals, from the very first issue to the very last, whatever portal they are distributed on. Thus, without having to change the interface, our readers can browse through the summaries of all editions of a journal, regardless of its access portal. However, if they wish to read the full text, they go through the document's original portal. They need only click on the title of an article in the summary to go directly to its page on its distribution portal. Hence, the reader can navigate amongst the various editions of a journal between the two portals. This interoperability is based on the use of the protocol OAI-PMH (Open Archives Initiative Protocol for Metadata Harvesting) and the sharing of XML data models (METS and Dublin Core formats)."

The technological evolutions of the Web have heralded the end of "closed" proprietary application solutions, where data and users were limited to ranges of products designed and marketed by certain commercial companies. This trend toward openness can be seen both for personal applications, which offer open document formats, and for CMSs and database management systems, which facilitate the importing/exporting of data from/to other products/devices.

In theory, the adaptability of these technologies renders the local logics of design of information systems accessible to the overall approaches of information meta-systems (engines, directories and syndication platforms), which use automatic processing to pool myriad documents in open formats. While meta-engines highlight the plasticity and evolutivity of the computer technologies used to harvest data from the Web, the issue of visibility of the organizational framework of the data is somewhat mistreated – or ignored – by Web harvesting and indexing tools. No matter how sophisticated the statistical and/or linguistic technique, these systems employ to order the responses and provide the Internaut with links to the most meaningful, relevant documents, the context of organization of the documents (and their status) and the way in which they are grouped together are insufficiently taken into consideration. This is demonstrated particularly well by digital audiovisual resources.

Audiovisual resource distribution platforms such as DailyMotion, YouTube, Vimeo, etc., have demonstrated that the technological procedures of searching in audiovisual (AV) content have remained crude in comparison to the sophistication of the techniques and search algorithms employed by the generalist search engines on textual documents [PAP 14b, STO 12, CHI 07, GRA 07]. Although considerable scientific progress has been made in terms of automated content analysis of video and audio (signal processing, vector-coding), the devices for indexing and searching in video-resources and audio resources remain of only experimental use on relatively small corpora which are not comparable to the AV resources available for consultation on the Web [PIG 12, GRO 05, LEF 03].

In practice, recent document portals (Persee, Cerimes, Gallica, Europeana, etc.) illustrate the delicacy of a position between tried-and-trusted knowledge-organization systems (which constitute invaluable tools for discovery of the collections) and the powerful information-seeking mechanisms of Web search engines, which are able to quickly compute candidate resource deemed to be relevant.

Internally, these documentary portals offer users both modes of searching: interrogation and exploration. When the Internaut chooses interrogation, he/she is aware of the generic organizational structure of the site (semiotic identity) – even if that awareness is only partial. In addition, the results returned by the portal's internal search engine refer to a set of structural characteristics of the site. On the other hand, when the results are provided by a generalist search engine (which has been able to exploit some of the metadata present in the digital documents on the portal), the whole organizational context of the documents is hidden from the Internaut (these aspects are particularly clear with Persee.fr, which offers extremely sophisticated search mechanisms and exploration mechanisms within the site itself, and also results that are produced by Google, which also indexes the digital resources of Persee.fr).

## 4.5. Rethinking the role of digital libraries

The documentary world of libraries appears as a largely-standardized environment where indexing rules and cataloging rules, models and bibliographical formats ensure the permanence of the collections constructed. On the other hand, the "digital library" is still struggling to find a stable definition, so changeable is the technological field in which it is rooted, and where the discriminating elements are found [CON 08, LAG 05]. However, the continuous evolution of ICT, which involves a constant cycle of the phases of innovation and obsolescence, condemns any attempt at formal characterization based on a technological state-of-the-art to a rapid death.

Numerous completed projects, which were all innovative at the time of their creation, bear witness to this: the Bibliothèque Universelle (Universal Library) built by the ABU (world book-lovers' association) intended to encourage the development and promotion of digital support; the institutional digital library Gallica, which offers free access to thousands of digitized books and images to any and all Internauts; the institutional open-archive depot of the CNRS, HAL (HyperArticles en Ligne – Online Hyperarticles), which is presented as a tool of direct communication between researchers; Wikipedia, the free encyclopedia, which contains millions of articles and has popularized the participative model; the institutional portal Persée, the earliest version of which imposed a moderated participative model (through forums) on digitized journals; revues.org, which constitutes an open electronic publication platform; and so on.

Indubitably, these documentary devices have made a significant contribution to the concept of a "digital library", but they have also blurred its boundaries, by introducing subordination of the use of ICT and by immediate transitivity to their dynamic of constant innovation. Hence, "The concept of a 'digital library' is an unstable compound, and, to a large extent, is a fantasy (…) Examining the possible uses of digital libraries should help us to come back a little from the realm of fantasy" [ROL 06]. It is surprising to note that the context of development of the digital libraries correlates so little to the context of its uses. Although these devices are essentially designed for the end user, usage studies aimed at measuring the usability and acceptability of these documentary artifacts are rare and do not fit in well with the unbridled cycle of "innovation/obsolescence". The multiplication of these digital documentation spaces, developed without any real visibility of the uses and non-uses, leads to the well-known issues highlighted by cognitive and informational analyses/studies [CHE 05, CAS 96].

## 4.6. Utopia of deintermediation in digital libraries

The amalgamation – and wholesale incorporation into the great "digital whole" [BER 08] – of documentary concerns is very distinct and relates to the publication, validation, collaboration and cowriting, organization and dissemination of knowledge, archiving, usage, accessibility, ergonomics, intellectual property, etc. [PED 06, CHA 06b]. It has finally led to the emergence of a simplistic two-pole schema: on the one hand, we have depots of digital and digitized documents, and on the other hand we have the potential users of that documentation. To begin with, this schema conveys the model of faultless ICT efficiency (computer applications, hardware, document formats, networks, etc.) for the *ex-nihilo* production of digital content and/or the conversion of paper documents (text supports, images and photographs) and audiovisual documents into enhanced digital avatars. However, on the flip side of the coin, there is an undeniable documentary deintermediation [ESP 03, BOR 01, VIE 97], where the typical user is modeled as having all the cognitive and instrumental abilities necessary for computer-assisted information mining [DIN 08, DES 06, DEN 06, FON 05].

While "digital library" initiatives usually arise from heritage-related actions (e.g. Gallica, Europeana, the Lisieux electronic library, the Centre Virtuel de la Connaissance sur l'Europe (Virtual Center of Knowledge about Europe), the INHA digital library, etc.), numerous operational projects to compose organized depots of digital content pertain to the world of higher education and research (Persée, HAL, Erudit, ArchiveSIC, Archives Audiovisuelles de la Recherche, revues.org, CAIRN, CERIMES, etc.). These autonomous information devices for the acquisition, organization and dissemination of digital content appear in an ambiguous light from an organizational standpoint. While, like all university libraries, their purpose is to offer support to higher education and research, in reality they only occupy a delicate position and relative visibility in the already highly-complex documentary systems of university libraries, which have arisen in accordance with the functions, profiles and curriculum of the users, with the constant aim of accessibility [COT 07, PAP 07b].

The editorial, technological, scientific or institutional aspirations at the heart of these depots and other digital archives have led to their development as distinct entities and autonomous systems, independently of the major axes of documentary policy which, in various establishments, define the acquisition of means and resources, the valuing of the collections, the training of personnel, the monitoring of research, services to the public, evaluation, etc.

These achievements therefore necessitate the irreversible establishment of a process of deintermediation where the role of the librarian is gradually eclipsed in favor of an interaction instrumented by ICT, placing the user in direct contact with heterogeneous documentary resources. The expression "digital library", which is gradually coming to substitute the appropriate formulations "electronic documentation", "digital collections", "digital resources" or "digital library services", feeds an incorrect idea of the technological situation of digital documents and their accessibility. Indeed, the expression suggests that digital depots of information (in the broadest sense) are founded on principles of organization of knowledge inherited from physical libraries, whereas the reality is totally different. Libraries, by adopting a given classification system (Universal Decimal Classification, Dewey Decimal Classification, Library of Congress system, etc.), in a given place, make the organization of their collections "intellectually compatible" with all other libraries employing the same system.

"Digital libraries", and their technological platforms, are far from being able to offer that same "operational standardization" of organization of digital resources. While the search tools (in the strictest sense) are very similar from one technical environment to another (all of them offer simple searches and advanced searches based on the rules of Boolean logic), they can only truly be used by a very small proportion of the users best trained in computerized document-mining techniques. The vast majority of users only make very limited use of the sophisticated search mechanisms, and soon run into the problems of noise and document silence. There is still a long way to go to endow the numerous digital libraries with that true technological, cognitive and cultural interoperability that their designers feel has been fully achieved.

A great deal of the research carried out by Pierre Rabardel, professor in psychology and ergonomics, has been based on a capable, pragmatic and active subject, who, by causing transformations in the real world, inevitably ends up modifying him/herself. This capacity for transformation corresponds to the power to act on the material world, which involves a work activity that cannot be dissociated from the use of material or symbolic instruments. This close relationship between the working activity and the instrument alters the forms of organization of the work performed by the instrument, and simultaneously modifies its functions. This evolution then contributes to the refinement of an instrument adapted for the subject's constructive activities.

ICT offers the possibility of strategic use of information because it can be controlled and manipulated – for example, by modifying the conditions of mutual enrichment of different information sources. By having access to quality resources and instruments appropriate for their constructive activities, civilian-Internauts have the power to select, filter and organize them. The results of these constructive actions, in addition to confirming the sense of an activity, because of the satisfaction that the activity produces, generate an increase in the power to act, which can then be reinvested in the activity.

The mechanisms of interoperability employed in digital libraries are generally envisaged solely in terms of their technological dimension, which their designers endow with the power to influence the digital uses and to make use of the digital collections. This system-oriented design, built on the imagined virtues of computer organization, does not entail the intended uses. This technological conjunction of interoperability, removed from the globalizing dimension of usage, thus leads to a twofold failure: first that of a free-to-access documentary service, which is unknown, in spite of the digital accessibility which would lead us to expect the opposite; and then that of a missed meeting with "civilian" Internauts, who are still on the outside of a device that they are unable to appropriate and which should serve their needs to link and contextualize information within that complex "Information Society" which develops new requirements of citizenship in their place.

Web technologies have reached an undeniable level of maturity in terms of performance and robustness, as is staunchly indicated by the presence of digital libraries. These Web technologies, which are interoperability technologies as understood by Berners-Lee, are capable of fully delivering the Memex, NLS and Xanadu Project conceived by Bush, Engelbart and Nelson.

By subjecting these technodocumentary architectures to usage logics devoted to surpassing the documentary perimeter of each of the digital libraries, it is possible to greatly increase the Internauts' ability to act: "The learning of knowledge needs to become active: we must listen, discuss, reorder, dissect, question the validity of the information presented, compare our knowledge with that of others, and reflect rather that assimilate. New technologies should enable us to rethink the act of learning (…). Education, but also professional and personal training, must no longer involve merely learning the content, but also learning methods of work, acquisition and manipulation of knowledge: those methods must privilege reflection about the information, and contrasting of knowledge and ideas" [RIC 96, p. 240].

# Bibliography

[AMB 05] AMBLARD P., *Régulation de l'Internet: L'élaboration des règles de conduite par le dialogue internormatif*, Emile Bruylant, Brussels, 2005.

[AMB 06] AMBLARD P., "Le droit d'auteur au service d'un partage maîtrisé des contenus en ligne", *Bulletin des bibliothèques de France*, no. 5, pp. 44–48, 2006.

[AMG 08] AMGHAR Y., "Documents Web 2.0", *Document numérique*, vol. 11, nos. 1–2, 2008.

[AND 05] ANDRÉ F., *Libre accès aux savoirs*, Futuribles, Paris, 2005.

[AND 06] ANDRADE BOTELHO DE ALMEIDA R., CUBAUD P., DUPIRE J. *et al.*, "Métadonnées et interactions riches pour les bibliothèques numérisées", *Document numérique*, vol. 9, no. 2, pp. 83–109, 2006.

[AND 12] ANDRO M., ASSELIN E., MAISONNEUVE M., *Bibliothèques numériques: logiciels et plateformes*, ADBS, Paris, 2012.

[ANG 11] ANGÉ C. (ed.), "Empreintes de l'hypertexte", *Les Cahiers du numérique*, vol. 3–4, 2011.

[ANT 04] ANTONIOU G., VAN HARMELEN F., *A Semantic Web Primer*, MIT Press, 2004.

[ANT 10] ANTONENKO P., NIEDERHAUSER D.S., "The influence of leads on cognitive load and learning in a hypertext environment", *Computers in Human Behavior*, no. 26, pp. 140–150, 2010.

[ARN 06] ARNAUD M., "Propriété intellectuelle et accès public au savoir en ligne", *Hermes*, vol. 45, 2006.

[ARP 10] ARPAGIAN N., "Internet et les réseaux sociaux: outils de contestation et vecteurs d'influence?", *Revue internationale et stratégique*, no. 78, pp. 97–102, 2010.

[ASS 02] ASSADI H., BEAUDOUIN V., "Comment utilise-t-on les moteurs de recherche sur Internet?", *Réseaux*, no. 116, pp. 171–198, 2002.

[ASS 07] ASSAR S., BOUGHZALA I. (eds), *Administration électronique. Constats et pespectives*, Hermes-Lavoisier, 2007.

[AUB 03] AUBERTIN G., BOUGHZALA I., ERMINE J.L., "Cartographie de connaissances critiques", in HACID M.-S., KODRATOFF Y., BOULANGER D. (eds), *Extraction et gestion des connaissances*, Lavoisier, vol. 17, nos. 1–3, 2003.

[BAC 04] BACCINO T., COLOMBI T., "Exploration visuelle et navigation dans les hypertextes: quelles stratégies?", *Ergo'IA*, Biarritz, 2004.

[BAC 09] BACHIMONT B., "Archivage audiovisuel et numérique: les enjeux de la longue durée", in LEBLOND C. (ed.), *Archivage et stockage pérenne. Enjeux et réalisations*, Hermes-Lavoisier, Paris, 2009.

[BAL 96] BALPE J.-P., LELU A., SALEH I. *et al.*, *Techniques avancées pour l'hypertexte*, Hermes, 1996.

[BAN 10] BANAT-BERGER F., "Les archives et la révolution numérique", *Le Débat*, vol. 1, no. 158, pp. 70–82, 2010.

[BAR 96] BARON L., TAGUE-SUTCLIFFE J., KINNUCAN M.T. *et al.*, "Labeled, typed links as cues when reading hypertext documents", *Journal of the Association for Information Science and Technology (JASIST)*, vol. 47, no. 12, pp. 896–908, 1996.

[BAR 07] BARCENILLA J., "De l'utilisabilité à l'acceptabilité: une approche multidimensionnelle de l'ergonomie des produits", *42ème congrès de la SELF*, pp. 423–429, 2007.

[BEA 02] BEAUVISAGE T., ASSADI H., "Les annuaires du Web", *Réseaux*, vol. 116, no. 6, pp. 141–170, 2002.

[BEA 07] BEARMAN D., "Digital libraries", *Ann. Rev. Info. Sci. Tech.*, no. 41, pp. 223–272, 2007.

[BEG 00] BEGUIN P., RABARDEL P., "Concevoir pour les activités instrumentées", *Revue d'Intelligence Artificielle*, vol. 14, nos. 1–2, pp. 35–54, 2000.

[BEG 05] BÉGUEC A., Evolution de la mise en espace des connaissances dans des médiathèques de dernière génération, Thesis, University of Lyon, 2005.

[BER 67] BERTIN J., *La sémiologie graphique*, Gauthier-Villars, Paris, 1967.

[BER 98] BERNERS-LEE T., Principles of design, available at: http://www.w3.org/DesignIssues/Principles.html, 1998.

[BER 06] BERENDT B., HOTHO A., MLADENIC D. *et al.* (eds), "From web to social web: discovering and deploying user and content profiles", *WebMine*, Berlin, 2006.

[BER 08] BERRY G., *Pourquoi et comment le monde devient numérique*, Collège de France, Fayard, 2008.

[BER 12] BERTHIER S., Le SIGB: pilier ou élément désormais mineur de l'informatique documentaire, Thesis, University of Lyon, January 2012.

[BER 13] BERMÈS E., *Le web sémantique en bibliothèque*, Le Cercle de la Librairie, Paris, 2013.

[BIG 12] BIGOT R., CROUTTE P., *La diffusion des technologies de l'information et de la communication dans la société française*, CREDOC, 2012.

[BIZ 11] BIZER C., HEALTH T., BERNERS-LEE T., "Linked data: the story so far", in SHETH A., HERSHEY P.A. (eds), *Semantic Services, Interoperability and Web Applications: Emerging Concepts*, Information Science Reference, 2011.

[BON 12] BONICEL M., "Hypertexte et manuscrits. Le défi de l'interopérabilité", *Revue de la BNF*, no. 42, pp. 22–28, March 2012.

[BOR 99] BORGMAN C.L., "What are digital libraries? Competing visions information", *Processing and Management*, no. 35, pp. 227–243, 1999.

[BOR 04] BORGMAN C.L., *The Interaction of Community and Individual Practices in the Design of a Digital Library*, Center for Embedded Network Sensing, 2004.

[BOR 01] BORGMAN C.L., "Where is the librarian in the digital library?", *Comm. of the ACM*, vol. 44, no. 5, pp. 66–67, 2001.

[BOU 03] BOURGEOIS F., EMPTOZ H., TRINH E. *et al.*, "Compression et accessibilité aux images de documents numérisés", *Document numérique*, vol. 7, pp. 103–125, March 2003.

[BOU 04] BOUKOTTAYA A., VANOIRBEEK C., PAGANELLI F. *et al.*, "Automating XML documents transformations: a conceptual modelling based approach", *Proceedings of the 1st Asian-Pacific Conference on Conceptual Modelling*, Australian Computer Society Inc., Dunedin, New Zealand, vol. 31, 2004.

[BOU 06] BOURMAUD G., Les systèmes d'instruments: méthodes d'analyse et perspectives de conception, PhD Thesis, University of Paris 8, 2006.

[BOU 09a] BOURGEAUX L., FRESNEAU A., "Moteur ou labyrinthe? Le portail documentaire de la bibliothèque publique d'information évalué par ses utilisateurs. Le patrimoine passe au numérique", *Bulletin des Bibliothèques de France*, Paris, vol. 54, no. 6, pp. 73–77, 2009.

[BOU 09b] BOUTET A., TRÉMEMBER J., "Mieux comprendre les situations de non-usages des TIC. Le cas d'Internet et de l'Informatique. Réflexions méthodologiques sur les indicateurs de l'exclusion dite numérique", *Les Cahiers du Numérique*, vol. 5, no.1, pp. 69–100, 2009.

[BOU 10] BOUQUILLION P., MATTHEWS J., *Le Web collaboratif*, Grenoble, PUG, 2010.

[BOU 11] BOUDOKHANE L.F., "Étude sur les non-usagers d'Internet: analyse de la perception des TIC et du rapport aux médias", *Les Enjeux de l'information et de la communication*, pp. 2–18, January 2011.

[BOU 13] BOUSTANY J., CHAMOUX J.-P., "Données publiques. Accès et usages", *Les Cahiers du Numérique*, vol. 9, no. 1, 2013.

[BOW 99] BOWKER G.C., STAR S.L., *Sorting Things Out: Classification and Its Consequences*, MIT Press, 1999.

[BRA 12] BRANGIER É. *et al.*, "Effets des personnes et contraintes fonctionnelles sur l'idéation dans la conception d'une bibliothèque numérique", *Le travail humain*, vol. 75, pp. 121–145, February 2012.

[BRO 88] BROWN P.J., "Hypertext: the way forward", in VAN VLIET J.C. (ed.), *Document Manipulation and Typography*, Combridge University Press, 1988.

[BRO 07] BROSSAUD C., REBER B., *Humanités numériques*, Hermes-Lavoisier, Paris, 2007.

[BRU 03] BRUILLARD E., DE LA PASSARDIÈRE B., "Ressources numériques, XML et education", *Sciences et Techniques Educatives*, 2003.

[BUC 97] BUCKLAND M., "What is a document?", *Journal of the Association for Information Science and Technology (JASIST)*, vol. 48, no. 9, pp. 804–809, 1997.

[BUR 96] BURBULES N.C., "Knowledge at the crossroads: some alternative futures of hypertext learning environments", *Educational Theory*, vol. 46, no. 1, pp. 23–50, 1996.

[BUS 45] BUSH V., "As we may think", *The Atlantic Monthly*, vol. 176, pp. 101–108, July 1945.

[CAL 07] CALÉ S., TOUITOU P., *La sécurité informatique: réponses techniques, organisationnelles et juridiques*, Hermes-Lavoisier, Paris, 2007.

[CAS 96] CASTELLI C., "Getting lost in hyperspace: lessons learned and future direction", *ED-MEDIA 96*, ED-TELECOM, 1996.

[CAS 11] CASEMAJOR-LOUSTAU N., "La contribution triviale des amateurs sur le Web: quelle efficacité documentaire?", *Études de communication*, no. 36, pp. 39–52, January, 2011.

[CAT 01] CATELLIN S., "Sérendipité, abduction et recherche sur Internet. Emergences et continuité dans les recherches en information et communication", *Actes du XIIe Congrès national des SIC, UNESCO*, SFSIC, Paris, 2001.

[CEN 99] CEN, Interoperability of health care multimedia report systems, CR Report no. 14300, 1999.

[CER 04] CERF M., "Intégrer les usages dans la conception ou concevoir dans l'usage? Construire la participation des utilisateurs dans les projets de conception", *Congrès SELF*, Geneva, 2004.

[CHA 89] CHARTRON G., DALBIN S., MONTEIL M.-G. *et al.*, "Indexation manuelle et indexation automatique: dépasser les oppositions", *Documentaliste-SI*, vol. 26, nos. 4–5, pp. 181–187, 1989.

[CHA 01] CHANCE M., *Les penseurs de fer. Les sirènes de la cyberculture*, Trait d'Union-Spirale, 2001.

[CHA 02a] CHAUDIRON S., L'évaluation des systèmes de traitement de l'information textuelle: vers un changement de paradigme, Thesis, University of Paris 10, Nanterre, 2002.

[CHA 02b] CHAMBERS P., IZAUTE M., MARESCAUX P.-J., *Metacognition: Process, Function and User*, Kluwer Academic Publishers, 2002.

[CHA 04] CHABIN A.-M., "Archivage et pérennisation", *Document numerique*, vol. 8, no. 2, Paris, 2004.

[CHA 06a] CHAUVIN S., Visualisations heuristiques pour la recherche et l'exploration de données dynamiques, PhD Thesis, University of Paris 8, 2006.

[CHA 06b] CHARTRON G., BROUDOUX E. (eds), *Document numérique et société*, ADBS, 2006.

[CHA 07a] CHANQUOY L., TRICOT J., SWELLER J., *La charge cognitive*, Armand Colin, 2007.

[CHA 07b] CHAUVIN S., PAPY F., SIDIR M. *et al.*, "Le portail institutionnel Persée à l'épreuve des usages. Croiser les approches méthodologiques en Sciences Humaines pour améliorer le partage de connaissances scientifiques en libre accès", *CAIS/ACSI Conference*, University of McGill, Montreal, Canada, 10–12 May 2007.

[CHE 04] CHEN S.Y., MAGOULA G.D., MACREDIE R.D., "Cognitive styles and users' responses to structured information representation", *Int. Journal Digital Library*, vol. 4, pp. 93–107, 2004.

[CHE 05] CHEVALIER A., TRICOT A. (eds), *Ergonomie des documents électroniques*, PUF, 2007.

[CHE 08] CHEVALIER A., "Pourquoi les sites Web sont-ils difficiles à utiliser? Quelques éléments de réponse", in CHEVALIER A., TRICOT A. (eds), *Ergonomie des documents électroniques*, PUF, 2008.

[CHE 11a] CHEN Y.-H., "Undergraduates' perceptions and use of the university libraries Web portal: can information literacy instruction make a difference?", *Proc. Am. Soc. Info. Sci. Tech.*, no. 48, pp. 1–10, 2011.

[CHE 11b] CHEVRY E., *Stratégies numériques*, Hermes-Lavoisier, Paris, 2011.

[CHE 12] CHEVRY PÉBAYLE E. (ed.), "Valorisation des corpus numérisés", *Les Cahiers du Numérique*, vol. 8, no. 2, p. 164, 2012.

[CHI 07] CHIARAMELLA Y., MULHEM P., "La recherche d'information. De la documentation automatique à la recherche d'information en contexte", *Document numérique*, pp. 11–38, 2007.

[CHI 08] CHICOINE P., "La bibliothèque 2.0 émerge à Québec", *Argus*, vol. 37, no. 2, 2008.

[CHR 02] CHRISTOFFEL M., SCHMITT B., "Accessing digital libraries as easy as a game", *Proceedings of the 2nd International Workshop on Visual Interfaces for Digital Libraries*, Portland, Oregon, 2002.

[CIA 05] CIACCIA A., MARTINS D., "Recherche d'informations sur le Web: étude de l'influence des facteurs liés à l'interface, à l'utilisateur et à la tâche", *Revue d'Intelligence Artificielle*, vol. 19, pp. 159–178, 2005.

[CLE 07] CLEMENT J., "L'hypertexte, une technologie intellectuelle à l'ère de la complexité", in BROSSAUD C., REBER B. (eds), *Humanités numériques 1*, Hermes-Lavoisier, Paris, 2007.

[COH 07] COHEN L.B., *Library 2.0 Initiatives in Academic Libraries*, Assoc. of College & Research Libraries, 2007.

[CON 87] CONKLIN J., "Hypertext: an introduction and survey", *Computer*, vol. 20, pp. 17–41, September 1987.

[CON 00] CONALLEN J., *Concevoir des applications Web avec UML*, Eyrolles, Paris, 2000.

[CON 08] CONSALVI M., EILRICH, E., SILLAUME, G., "Rôles et perspectives des bibliothèques numériques dans l'économie de la connaissance: une étude de cas", *Colloque en route vers Lisbonne*, p. 9, Luxembourg, 2008.

[COR 82] CORSON Y., Aspects psychologiques liés a l'interrogation d'une base de données, INRIA Report, Rocquencourt, 1982.

[COT 07] COTTE D., "L'organisation des connaissances entre le formalisme des outils et la complexité des représentations: une illustration par le cas des portails d'entreprise", *ISKO Conference*, France, 2007.

[COU 97] COURBON J.-C., TAJAN S., *Groupware et intranet*, Eyrolles, Paris, 1997.

[COU 13] COUGHLIN D.M., CAMPBELL M.C., JANSEN B.J., "Measuring the value of library content collections", *Proc. Am. Soc. Info. Sci. Tech.*, no. 50, pp. 1–13, 2013.

[CRA 01] CRASSON A., "Genèse et hypertexte: échange de partitions", *Diogène*, no. 196, pp. 95–103, 2001.

[CUB 08] CUBAUD P., "Interaction for digital libraries," in PAPY F. (ed.), *Digital Libraries*, ISTE, London and John Wiley & Sons, New York, January 2008.

[DAC 90] DACHELET R., "Hypertexte et hypermédia: Documents – Informations – Connaissances", Le document électronique, course by Christian Bornes, pp. 135–161, 1990.

[DAV 99] DAVIS H.C., "Hypertext link integrity", *ACM Computing Surveys*, vol. 31, no. 4, December 1999.

[DAV 07] DAVIS P.M., CONNOLLY M.J.L., "Institutional repositories. Evaluating the reasons for non-use of Cornell University's installation of DSpace", *D-Lib Magazine*, vol. 13, nos. 3–4, March–April 2007.

[DEB 10] DEBOS F., "Piloter l'entreprise à l'ère du numérique", *Les Cahiers du Numérique*, vol. 6, no. 4, 2010.

[DEN 03] DENECKER C., *Les compétences documentaires: des processus mentaux à l'utilisation de l'information*, Presses de l'ENSSIB, Lyon, 2003.

[DEN 06] DENECKER C., KOLMAYER E., *Eléments de psychologie cognitive pour les sciences de l'information*, Presses de l'ENSSIB, 2006.

[DES 06] DESPRÉS-LONNET, M., COURTECUISSE, J.-F., "Les étudiants et la documentation électronique", *Bulletin des Bibliothèques de France*, no. 2, p. 33–41, 2006.

[DES 09] DESEILLIGNY O., "Pratiques d'écriture adolescentes: l'exemple des Skyblogs", *Le Journal des psychologues*, no. 272, pp. 30–35, September 2009.

[DEX 12] DEXTRE C., STELLA G., "ISO 25964: a standard in support of KOS interoperability", in GILCHRIST A., VERNAU J. (eds), *Facets of Knowledge Organization*, Emerald, London, 4–5 July 2012.

[DHA 09] D'HALLUIN C., DELACHE D., "Etude d'un processus dynamique de construction d'une communauté par interactions entre dispositif et interface numérique", in SIDIR M. (ed.), *La comunication éducative et les TIC*, Hermes-Lavoisier, Paris, pp. 101–122, 2009.

[DIN 02] DINET J., ROUET J.-F., "La recherche d'information: processus cognitifs, facteurs de difficultés et dimension de l'expertise", in PAGANELLI C. (ed.), *Interaction Homme-Machine et recherche d'information*, Hermes-Lavoisier, Paris, pp. 133–161, 2002.

[DIN 07] DINET J., VIVIAN R., "La recherche collaborative d'information. Vers un système centré utilisateur", *Document numérique*, vol. 10, nos. 3–4, pp. 25–46, 2007.

[DIN 08] DINET J., *Usages, usagers et compétences informationnelles au 21è siècle*, Hermes-Lavoisier, Paris, 2008.

[DIN 14] DINET J., *Information Retrieval in Digital Environments*, ISTE, London and John Wiley & Sons, New York, 2014.

[DIR 15] DIRECTION INTERMINISTERIELLE DES SYSTÈMES D'INFORMATION ET DE COMMUNICATION, Référentiel Général d'Interopérabilité. Standardiser, s'aligner et se focaliser pour échanger efficacement, version 1.9.7, March 2015.

[DUB 01] DUBEY G., *Le lien social à l'ère du virtuel*, Presses Universitaires de France, Paris, 2001.

[DOU 08] DOUEIHI M., *La grande conversion numérique*, Le Seuil, Paris, 2008.

[DUB 09] DUBOIS M., BOBILLIER-CHAUMON M.-E., "L'acceptabilité des technologies: bilans et nouvelles perspectives", *Le travail humain*, vol. 72, pp. 305–310, April 2009.

[DUC 02] DUCARD D., "De mémoire d'hypertexte", *Communication et langages*, no. 131, pp. 81–91, 2002.

[DUF 01] DUFOUR C., BERGERON P., "Lorsque systèmes d'information Web et professionnels de l'information se rencontrent", in CAMPBELL G. (ed.), *Proceedings of the 29th Annual Conference of the Canadian Association for Information Science*, 27–29 May 2001.

[DUJ 06] DUJOL A., "Les sites web des bibliothèques. Trouver l'information ou la ronde des clics", *Bulletin des Bibliothèques de France*, vol. 51, no. 3, pp. 38–42, 2009.

[ENG 62] ENGELBART D.C., Augmenting human intellect: a conceptual framework, Summary Report AF 49(638)-1024, Stanford Research Institute, October 1962.

[ESC 10] ESCHENFELDER K.R., CASWELL M., "Digital cultural collections in an age of reuse and remixes", *Proc. Am. Soc. Info. Sci. Tech.*, no. 47, pp. 1–10, 2010.

[ESP 03] ESPAIGNET S., FOFANA R., LAURENCEAU A., Pertinence de l'idée de désintermédiation documentaire, Research Report, DCB University of Lyon, 2003.

[EUR 06] EUROPEAN UNION, Recommandation 2006/962/CE du Parlement européen et du Conseil, du 18 décembre 2006, sur les compétences clés pour l'éducation et la formation tout au long de la vie, available at: eur-lex.europa.et, 2006.

[FAR 08] FARGIER N., NÉOUZE V., "Persée, un outil au service de la communication scientifique francophone", *World Library and Information Congress, 74th IFLA General Conference and Council*, Quebec, Canada, 10–14 August 2008.

[FAV 13] FAVIER L., MUSTAFA EL HADI W., "L'interopérabilité des systèmes d'organisation des connaissances: une nouvelle conception de l'universalité du savoir?", in PAPY F. (ed.), *Recherches Ouvertes sur le numérique*, Hermes-Lavoisier, Paris, 2013.

[FEK 06] FEKETE J.D., LECOLINET E., "Visualisation pour les bibliothèques numériques", *Document numérique*, vol. 9, no. 2, 2006.

[FEY 07] FEYLER F., "De la compatibilité à l'interopérabilité en matière de repérage d'information pertinente", *Documentaliste-SI*, vol. 44, pp. 84–92, January 2007.

[FLI 04] FLICHY P., DAGIRAL E., "L'administration électronique: une difficile mise en cohérence des acteurs", *Revue française d'administration publique*, no. 110, pp. 245–255, 2004.

[FOL 03] FOLCHER V., "Appropriating artifacts as instruments: when design-for-use meets design-in use", in *Interacting with Computers*", 2003.

[FOL 05] FOLCHER V., SANDER E., "Usages, appropriation: analyse sémantique a priori et analyse de l'activité instrumentale", in RABARDEL P., PASTRÉ P. (eds), *Modèles du sujet pour la conception*, Octares, 2005.

[FON 05] FONDIN H., "La formation à la recherche d'information: préoccupation citoyenne ou vision obsolète", *Esquisse*, no. 43, p. 16, 2005.

[FRA 08] FRANCE NUMERIQUE 2012, Plan de développment de l'écenomie numérique, available at: www.francenumerique2012.fr, 2008.

[FRE 95] FREI H.P., STIEGER D., "The use of semantic links in hypertext information retrieval", *Information Processing & Management*, vol. 31, no. 1, pp. 1–13, 1995.

[FRE 13] FREYRE E., "TEL and Europeana: thematic examples of cooperation between cultural institutions", *European Seminar of the PhD School in Human and Society Sciences,* University of Lille 3, 12 April 2013.

[GAR 99] GARLATTI S., IKSAL S., "Documents virtuels personnalisables pour des systèmes d'informations en ligne", *Workshop sur les Documents Virtuels Personnalisables IHM'99*, Montpellier, pp. 22–26, 1999.

[GAR 03] GARDEY D., "De la domination à l'action. Quel genre d'usage des technologies de l'information", *Réseaux*, no. 120, pp. 87–117, 2003.

[GAR 08] GARDNER GROUP, Cloud computing: defining and describing an emerging phenomenon, available at: http://www.gardner.com, 17 June 2008.

[GAZ 08] GAZO D., "Le Web 2.0 et les bibliothèques 2.0", available at: http://bibliodoc.francophonie.org, 2008.

[GER 01] GERMAIN M., "Evolution de l'utilisation de l'intranet dans les entreprises", *Réseaux humains/réseaux technologiques*, pp. 59–78, 19 May 2001.

[GER 05] GERHARD M., BUURMAN M. (eds), *Total Interaction. Theory and Practice of a New Paradigm for the Design Disciplines*, Birkhäuser, Basel, Switzerland, 2005.

[GER 06] GEROIMENKO V., CHEN C., *Visualizing the Semantic Web: XML-based Internet and Information Visualization*, Birkhäuser, 2006.

[GES 02] GESLIN P., "Les formes sociales d'appropriations des objets techniques, ou le paradigme anthropotechnologique", *ethnographiques.org*, no. 1, April 2002.

[GHI 02] GHITALLA F., "L'âge des cartes électroniques. Outils graphiques de navigation sur le Web", *Communication et Langages*, no. 131, 2002.

[GIV 03] GIVEN L., OLSON H.O., "Knowledge organization in research: a conceptual model for organizing data", *Library & Information Science Research*, vol. 25, pp. 157–176, 2003.

[GOL 97] GOLOVCHINSKY G., "What the query told the link: the integration of hypertext and information retrieval", *Hypertext 97 ACM*, Southampton, UK, pp. 67–75, 1997.

[GON 04] GONÇALVES M.A., Streams, structures, spaces, scenarios and societies: a formal framework for digital libraries and its applications, PhD Thesis, Virginia Tech CS Department, 2004.

[GON 07] GONÇALVES M.A., MOREIRA B.L., FOX E.A. *et al.*, "What is a good digital library? A quality model for digital libraries", *Information Processing & Management*, vol. 43, no. 5, pp. 1416–1437, September 2007.

[GRA 07] GRAU B., CHEVALLET J.-P., *La recherche d'informations précises: traitement automatique de la langue, apprentissage et connaissances pour les systèmes de question-réponse*, Hermes-Lavoisier, Paris, 2007.

[GRA 11] GRANITZER M., LINDSTAEDT S., "Semantic web: theory and applications", *Journal of Universal Computer Science*, vol. 17, no. 7, pp. 981–982, 2011.

[GRA 13] GRACY K.F., LEI ZENG M., SKIRVIN L., "Exploring methods to improve access to music resources by aligning library data with linked data: a report of methodologies and prelimary findinds", *Journal of the Association for Information Science and Technology (JASIST)*, vol. 64, no. 10, pp. 2078–2099, 2013.

[GRI 11] GRIVEL L. (ed.), *La recherche d'information en contexte: Outils et usages applicatifs*, Hermes-Lavoisier, Paris, 2011.

[GRO 05] GROS P., "Description et indexation automatiques des documents multimédias: du fantasme à la réalité", *Documentaliste-Sciences de l'Information*, vol. 42, no. 6, pp. 383–391, 2005.

[GRO 07] GROS P. (ed.), *L'indexation multimédia. Description et recherche automatiques*, Hermes-Lavoisier, Paris, 2007.

[GUE 10] GUEGAN A., Valorisation des ressources pédagogiques en ligne au SCD de l'Université de Limoges: le cas des Universités Numériques Thématiques, Thesis, University of Lyon, March 2010.

[GUN 13] GUNS R., "Tracing the origins of the semantic web", *Journal of the Association for Information Science and Technology (JASIST)*, vol. 64, no. 10, pp. 2173–2181, 2013.

[HAL 11] HALPIN H., LAVRENKO V., "Relevance feedback between hypertext and semantic web search: frameworks and evaluation", *Web Semantics: Science, Services and Agents on the World Wide Web*, no. 9, pp. 474–489, 2011.

[HAR 13] HAREJ V., ŽUMER M., "Analysis of FRBR user tasks", *Cataloging & Classification Quarterly*, vol. 51, no. 7, pp. 741–759, 2013.

[HAS 04] HASCOËT M., "Visualisation d'information et interaction", in IHADJADENE M. (ed.), *Méthodes avancées pour les systèmes de recherche d'informations*, Hermes-Lavoisier, Paris, 2004.

[HEN 14] HENOCQUE B., CONTE B., "Problématiques juridiques et technologies numériques", *Les Cahiers du Numériques*, vol. 10, February 2014.

[HER 13] HERON S.J., SIMPSON B., WEISS A.K. *et al.*, "Bibliographic environment for the State University Libraries of Florida", *Cataloging & Classification Quarterly*, vol. 51, nos. 1–3, pp. 139–155, 2013.

[HEW 90] HEWIJNEN (VAN) E., *Practical SGML*, Kluwer Academic Publishers, 1990.

[HOC 06] HOCHEREAU F., "Concrétisation et normalisation: l'injonction contradictoire de l'inscription de l'informatique dans l'organisation", *Réseaux*, nos. 135–136, pp. 287–321, 2006.

[HOU 92] HOUDE O., *Catégorisation et développement cognitif*, PUF, Paris, 1992.

[HUD 12] HUDON M., "ISO25964: pour le développement, la gestion et l'interopérabilité des langages documentaires", *Documentation et bibliothèques*, vol. 3, no. 58, pp. 130–140, 2012.

[HUS 98] HUSTACHE-GODINET H., Lire-Ecrire des hypertextes, PhD Thesis, Université Stendhal Grenoble 3, 1998.

[IHA 04] IHADJADENE M., (coord.) *Les systèmes de recherche d'informations, modèles conceptuels*, Hermes-Lavoisier, Paris, 2004.

[IHA 08] IHADJADENE M., CHAUDIRON S., "Quelles analyses de l'usage des moteurs de recherche", *Questions de communication*, no. 14, 2008.

[ISO 98] ISO 9241-11, Ergonomic requirement for offices with visual display terminals (VDTs)–Part II: Guidance on usability, 1998.

[JAC 01] JACOB C., "Rassembler la mémoire. Réflexions sur l'histoire des bibliothèques", *Diogène*, no. 196, pp. 53–77, 2001.

[JAN 05] JANNÈS-OBER E., "L'usager face à la bibliothèque numérique: l'expérience du portail d'information scientifique de l'Institut Pasteur", in PAPY F. (ed.), *Les Bibliothèques Numériques*, Hermes-Lavoisier, Paris, 2005.

[JEA 00] JEANNERET Y., *Y a-t-il (vraiment) des Technologies de l'Information?*, Presses Universitaires du Septentrion, 2000.

[JOC 08] JOCHEMS S., RIVARD M., "TIC et citoyenneté: de nouvelles pratiques sociales dans la société de l'information", *Nouvelles Pratiques Sociales*, vol. 21, no. 1, pp. 1–182, 2008.

[JUL 03] JULIA J.-T., "Interactivité, modes d'emploi", *Documentaliste-Sciences de l'Information*, vol. 40, no. 3, pp. 204–212, 2003.

[KAR 07] KARI J., SAVOLAINEN R., "Relationships between information seeking and context: a qualitative study of Internet searching and the goals of personal development", *Library & Information Science Research*, vol. 29, pp. 47–69, 2007.

[KIY 09] KIYINDOU A. (ed.), "Fracture numérique et justice sociale", *Les Cahiers du Numérique*, vol. 5, no. 1, 2009.

[KOF 14] KOFORD A., "How disability studies scholars interact with subject headings", *Cataloging & Classification Quarterly*, vol. 52, no. 4, pp. 388–411, 2014.

[KOO 05] KOOHANG A., ONDRACEK J., "Users' views about the usability of digital libraries", *British Journal of Educational Technology*, no. 36, pp. 407–423, 2005.

[KOS 06] KOSHMAN S., SPINK A., JANSEN B.J. *et al.*, "Metasearch results visualization: an exploratory study", *Canadian Association for Information Science*, York University, Toronto, 1–3 June 2006.

[KOS 11] KOSZOWSKA-NOWAKOWSKA P., RENUCCI F., "L'hypertexte: approches expérimentale et herméneutique", *Les Cahiers du numérique*, vol. 7, pp. 71–91, March 2011.

[KUH 04] KUHLTHAU C.C., *Seeking Meaning: a Process Approach to Library and Information Services*, Libraries Unlimited, CT, 2004.

[KUN 96] KUNY T., CLEVELAND G., "Digital libraries: myths and challenges", *62nd IFLA General Conference*, 25–31 August 1996.

[LAG 05] LAGOZE C., KRAFFT D.B., PAYETTE S. *et al.*, "What is a digital library anyway, anymore?", *D-Lib Magazine*, vol. 11, November 2005.

[LAU 95] LAUFER R., SCAVETTA D., *Texte, hypertexte, hypermédia*, Presses Universitaires de France, Paris, 1995.

[LAU 02] LAUBLET P., NAÏT-BAHA L., JACKIEWICZ A. *et al.*, "Collecte d'informations textuelles sur le Web selon différents points de vue", in PAGANELLI C. (ed.), *IHM et recherche d'informations*, Hermes-Lavoisier, 2002.

[LEB 08] LEBRETON C., BIBLIOTHÈQUES T., FOLKSONOMIES, L'indexation des bibliothécaires à l'ère sociale, University of Lyon, March 2008.

[LEC 97] LE COADIC Y., *Usages et usagers de l'information*, ADBS, Nathan, 1997.

[LEE 03] LEE H.-L., "Information spaces and collections: implications for organization", *Library & Information Science Research*, no. 25, pp. 419–436, 2003.

[LEF 00] LEFÈVRE P., *La recherche d'informations. Du texte intégral au thésaurus*, Hermes, Paris, 2000.

[LEF 04] LEFÈVRE S., SÈDES F., "Indexation de séquences vidéo", *Document numérique*, vol. 8, pp. 41–48, April 2004.

[LEL 98] LELU A., Représentations cartographiques de corpus textuels: codages, algorithmes, ergonomie, Thesis, University of Paris 8, 1998.

[LEL 99] LELOUP C., *Moteurs d'indexation et de recherche*, Eyrolles, Paris, 1999.

[LEL 04a] LELEU-MERVIEL S., "Effets de la numérisation et de la mise en réseau sur le concept de document", *Information-Interaction-Intelligence*, Cépadues, Paris, vol. 4, no. 1, pp. 121–140, 2004.

[LEL 04b] LELONG B., THOMAS F., ZIEMLICKI C., "Des technologies inégalitaires? L'intégration de l'internet dans l'univers domestique et les pratiques relationnelles", *Réseaux*, nos. 127–128, pp. 141–180, 2004.

[LEM 90] LE MAREC J., *Dialogue ou labyrinthe? La consultation des catalogues informatisés par les usagers*, BPI, 1990.

[LEM 03] LE MONDE INFORMATIQUE, "Misez sur les technologies Web", PME-PMI, pp. 17–38, 21 November 2003.

[LET 14] LETROUVÉ F., MAISONNEUVE M., "Méthodes, techniques et outils. Un Web accessible: accessibilité numérique pour certains, qualité et confort pour tous!", *Documentaliste-SI*, vol. 51, no. 32, pp. 14–16, June 2014.

[LEV 98] LEVINE J.R., BAROUDI C., *Internet: les fondamentaux*, Vuibert Informatique, International Thomson Publication, Paris, 1998.

[LEW 08] LEWANDOWSKI D., HÖCHSTÖTTER N., "Mesurer la qualité des moteurs de recherche Web", *Questions de communication*, vol. 14, pp. 75–93, 2008.

[LIN 13] LINDQUIST T., DULOCK M., TÖRNROOS J. *et al.*, "Using linked open data to enhance subject access in online primary sources", *Cataloging & Classification Quarterly*, vol. 51, no. 8, pp. 913–928, 2013.

[LOM 07] LOMPRÉ N., "Normes ergonomiques et usages des bibliothèques numériques", in PAPY F. (ed.), *Usages et pratiques dans les bibliothéques numériques*, Hermes-Lavoisier, Paris, 2007.

[LUP 07] LUPOVICI C., "Les usages des bibliothèques numériques: de Gallica à Europeana", *53 ème congrès de l'ABF*, Nantes, p. 7, 8–11 June 2007.

[MAD 09] MADRID R.I., VAN OOSTENDORP H., PUERTA MELGUIZO M.C., "The effects of the number of links and navigation support on cognitive load and learning with hypertext: The mediating role of reading order" *Computer in Human Behavior*, vol. 25, no. 1, pp. 66–75, 2009.

[MAG 95] MAGNE N., Henri Lemaître 1881–1946. De la lecture publique à la documentation, Thesis, Panthéon-Sorbonne, University of Paris, 1995.

[MAL 02] MALLEIN P., TAROZZI S., "Des signaux d'usage pertinents pour la conception des objets communicants", *Les Cahiers du Numérique*, vol. 3, no. 4, pp. 61–70, 2002.

[MAN 00] MANDOSIO J.-M., *Après l'effondrement. Notes sur l'utopie néotechnologique*, Editions de l'Encyclopédie des Nuissances, Paris, 2000.

[MAN 99] MANDOSIO J.-M., *L'effondrement de la très grande bibliothèque nationale de France: Ses causes, ses conséquences*, Editions de l'Encyclopédie des Nuissances, Paris, 1999.

[MAN 02] MANIEZ J., *Actualité des langages documentaires. Fondements théoriques de la recherche d'information*, ADBS, Paris, 2002.

[MAN 04] MANES-GALLO M.C., PAGANELLI C., "La recherche d'information assistée par ordinateur: quelle représentation des connaissances?", *Les enjeux de l'information et de la communication*, GRESEC, 2004.

[MAR 88] MARCHIONINI F., SHNEIDERMANN B., "Findings facts vs. browsing knowledge in hypertext systems", *Computer*, pp. 70–80, 1988.

[MAR 93] MARSHALL C.C., SHIPMAN M., "Searching for the missing link: discovering implicit structure in spatial hypertext", *HYPERTEXT '93, Proceedings of the 5th ACM Conference on Hypertext*, pp. 217–230, 1993.

[MAR 09] MARON N.L., KIRBY SMITH K., LOG M., "Sustaining digital resources: an on-the ground view of projects today", *JISC Content*, 2009.

[MAT 01] MATTELARD A., *Histoire de la société de l'Information*, La Découverte, Paris, 2001.

[MAT 05] MATHIEN M. (ed.), *La société de l'information*, Bruylant, Brussels, 2005.

[MAT 12] MATHIEU A. *et al.*, "Valoriser une bibliothèque numérique par des choix de référencement et de diffusion", *Les Cahiers du numérique*, vol. 8, no. 3, pp. 75–90, 2012.

[MCA 99] MCALEESE R. (ed.), *Hypertext. Theory into Practice*, Intellect, 1999.

[MCK 91] MCKNIGHT C., DILLON A., RICHARDSON J., *Hypertext in Context*, Cambridge University Press, 1991.

[MEY 09] MEYER T., "L'apprenant digital", *Médium*, no. 18, pp. 89–99, 2009.

[MIC 98] MICHARD A., *XML, langage et applications*, Eyrolles, Paris, 1998.

[MIE 03] MIÈGE B., *Communication personnes systèmes informationnels*, Hermes-Lavoisier, Paris, 2003.

[MIE 04] MIÈGE B., *L'information-communication, objet de connaissance*, De Boeck University, 2004.

[MIL 00] MILLER P., "Interoperability: what is it and why should I want it?", *Ariadne*, no. 24, June 2000.

[MOA 12] MOATTI A., "Bibliothèque numérique européenne: de l'utopie aux réalités", *Annales des mines – réalités industrielles*, pp. 43–46, 2012.

[MOE 98] MOEGLIN P., *L'industrialisation de la formation. Etat de la question*, CNDP, 1998.

[MOR 99] MORIN E., *Le défi du XXIe siècle: relier les connaissances*, Éditions du Seuil, 1999.

[MOR 08] MORRISON P.J., "Tagging and searching: search retrieval effectiveness of folksonomies on the world wide web", *Information Processing & Management*, vol. 44, no. 4, pp. 1562–1579, 2008.

[MUC 01] MUCCHIELLI A., *Les sciences de l'information et de la communciaiton*, Hachette, Paris, 2001.

[MUG 13] MUGRIDGE R.L., "The value of collaboration and partnerships in cataloging", *Cataloging & Classification Quarterly*, vol. 51, nos. 1–3, pp. 1–5, 2013.

[MUS 08] MUSSO P., ESPARRE S., CORDOBÈS S. *et al.*, *Territoires et cyberespace en 2030*, La Documentation française, 2008.

[MUS 10] MUSSO P., "De la socio-utopie à la techno-utopie", *Manière de voir*, no. 112, August–September 2010.

[NAN 93] NANARD J., NANARD M., "Should anchors be typed too? An experiment with MacWeb", *Proceedings of the 5th ACM Conference on Hypertext*, pp. 51–62, 1993.

[NAN 95] NANARD M., "Les hypertextes: au-delà des liens, la connaissance", *Sciences et techniques éducatives*, vol. 2, no. 1, pp. 31–59, 1995.

[NAU 00] Naudé G., A*dvis pour dresser une bibliothèque*, Phénix Editions, Paris, 2000.

[NEW 91] NEWCOMB S.R., KIPP N.A., NEWCOMB V.T., "The 'Hytime': hypermedia/time-based document structuring language", *CACM*, vol. 34, no. 11, pp. 67–83, 1991.

[NIC 08] NICOLAS Y., "Calames, et après?", *Bulletin des Bibliothèques de France*, Paris, vol. 53, no. 6, pp. 29–33, 2008.

[NIE 89] NIELSEN J., *Hypertext and Hypermedia*, Academic Press, 1989.

[NIE 90] NIELSEN J., "The art of navigating through hypertext", *ACM*, vol. 33, no. 3, pp. 298–310, 1990.

[NOË 97] NOËL B., *La métacognition*, De Boeck University, 1997.

[ONE 14] O'NEILL E.T., RICK BENNETT, "Using authorities to improve subject searches", *Cataloging & Classification Quarterly*, vol. 52, no. 1, pp. 6–19, 2014.

[ORE 05] O'REILLY T., What is Web 2.0? Design patterns and business models for the next generation of software, available at: http://www.oreillynet.com/, 30 September 2005.

[PAG 98] PAGE L., BRIN S., The anatomy of a large-scale hypertextual Web search engine, In: Seventh International World-Wide Web Conference, available at: http://infolab.stanford.edu/~backrub/google.html, Brisbane, Australia, April 14-18, 1998.

[PAN 96] PANSU A., "Organisation des collections dans l'espace", *Bulletin de l'Association des Bibliothécaires français*, no. 170, pp. 6–8, 1996.

[PAN 98] PANKO R.R., "Lessons from the first hypertext digital library, the NLS/augment journal system, a hypertext management system (HMS)", *System Sciences*, vol. 2, pp. 68 –172, 1998.

[PAN 14] PANESCU A.-T., SIMKO T., VANOIRBEEK C., "Targeted annotation of scientific literature and data resources in Invenio digital libraries", *Open Repositories*, Helsinki, Finland, 9–13 June, 2014.

[PAP 95] PAPY F., Hypertextualisation automatique de documents techniques, PhD Thesis, University of Paris 8, 1995.

[PAP 01] PAPY F., BOUHAÏ N., "Chercher et réorganiser l'information sur le Web", *Actes du 5ème coll. Hypermédias et Apprentissages*, Grenoble, pp. 49–58, 2001.

[PAP 03a] PAPY F., "De l'hypermédia aux contenus riches. Evolution des concepts", *Seminar material, École* Polytechnique, Paris, 30 January 2003.

[PAP 03b] PAPY F., BOUHAI N., "HyWebMap et K-Web Organizer: Dispositifs complémentaires d'organisation individuelle et communautaire de connaissances", *4eme Congrès ISKO-France*, Grenoble, 3–4 July 2003.

[PAP 04] PAPY F., FOLCHER V., SIDIR M. *et al.*, "E-Learning et technologies pour la coopération: inadéquations artefactuelles et logiques des activités instrumentées", *ERGO'IA*, Biarritz, 2004.

[PAP 05] PAPY F. (ed.), *Les bibliothèques numériques*, Hermes-Lavoisier, 2005.

[PAP 07a] PAPY F., LEBLOND C., "L'interface de recherche d'information du Visual Catalog: un outil innovant à double détente", *Documentaliste-SI*, vol. 44, nos. 4–5, pp. 288–298, 2007.

[PAP 07b] PAPY F. (ed.), *Usages et pratiques dans les bibliothèques numériques*, Hermes-Lavoisier, Paris, 2007.

[PAP 07c] PAPY F. (ed.), "Usages et numériques", *Document numérique*, December 2007.

[PAP 07d] PAPY F., SIDIR M., STOCKINGER P., "Le portail institutionnel Persée à l'épreuve des usages. Croiser les approches méthodologiques en Sciences Humaines pour améliorer le partage de connaissances scientifiques en libre accès", *CAIS/ACSI Conference*, University of McGill, Montréal, Canada, 2007.

[PAP 08] PAPY F. (ed.), *Problématiques émergentes dans les sciences de l'Information*, Hermes-Lavoisier, Paris, 2008.

[PAP 09] PAPY F., *Technodocumentation: des machines informationnelles aux bibliothèques numériques*, Hermes-Lavoisier, Paris, 2009.

[PAP 10] PAPILLOUD C., "L'interactivité", *tic&société*, vol. 4, no. 1, 2010.

[PAP 11] PAPY F., LEBLOND C., "Continuité documentaire du lycée à l'Université: résultats d'une expérimentation originale de formation à l'information entre documentalistes de lycées, bibliothécaires en universités et chercheurs en Sciences de l'Information", *3e Colloque Spécialisé en Sciences de l'Information (COSSI)*, University of Moncton, 8-9 June 2011.

[PAP 12] PAPY F. (ed.), *Evolutions sociotechniques des bibliothèques numériques*, Hermes-Lavoisier, Paris, 2012.

[PAP 14a] PAPY F., SANSONETTI D., *Les technologies du Web au défi de l'entreprise*, Hermes-Lavoisier, Paris, 2014.

[PAP 14b] PAPY F., STOCKINGER P., "Archives audiovisuelles numériques de la recherche en SHS et Digital Information Design: rencontre entre sémiotique de l'audiovisuelle numérique et nouvelles interfaces documentaires", *Echappées*, no. 2, pp. 28–36, 2014.

[PAR 02] PARK J., HUNTING S., *XML Topic Maps: Creating and Using Topic Maps for the Web*, Addison-Wesley Longman Publishing, Boston, MA, 2002.

[PAR 07] PARROCHIA D., "L'Internet et ses représentations", *Rue Descartes*, no. 55, 2007.

[PAV 89] PAVÉ F., *L'illusion informaticienne*, L'Harmattan, 1989.

[PED 06] PÉDAUQUE R. T., *Le document à la lumière du numérique*, C&F éditions, 2006.

[PED 07] PÉDAUQUE R.T., *La redocumentarisation du monde*, Cépaduès, 2007.

[PEN 08] PENICHON M., De la collaboration à la mutualisation entre bibliothèques municipales et universitaires: un nouveau modèle pour l'avenir, Thesis, University of Lyon, March 2008.

[PIE 14] PIÉGAY N., "Un bouleversement du rapport aux savoirs", *Documentaliste-Sciences de l'Information*, vol. 51, pp. 7–9, April 2014.

[PIG 06] PIGNIER N., "Pour une approche sémio-pragmatique de la communication", *Questions de communication*, pp. 419–433, 2006.

[PIG 12] PIGNIER N., "Le plaisir de l'interaction entre l'usager et les objets TIC numériques", *Interfaces numériques*, vol. 1, no. 1, pp. 123–152, 2012.

[PIN 07] PINON J.-M., BEIGBEDER M., "Recherche d'informations dans les documents structurés", *Document numérique*, vol. 10, 2007.

[PIR 10] PIROLLI P., "Web 2.0 et pratiques documentaires", *Les Cahiers du numérique*, vol. 6, no. 1, pp. 81–95, 2010.

[PLA 88] PLANCHE R., *Maîtriser la modélisation conceptuelle*, Masson, Paris, 1988.

[PLA 14] PLANTIN J.-C., *La cartographie numérique*, ISTE Editions, London, 2014.

[POL 98] POLLITT A.S., "The key role of classification and indexing in view-bases searching", *IFLA Council and General Conference* no. 63, Copenhagen, Denmark, vol. 27, no. 2, pp. 37–40, 1998.

[PRI 05] PRINTZ J., MESDON B., *Ecosystème des projets informatiques: agilité et discipline*, Hermes-Lavoisier, Paris, 2005.

[QUI 03] QUINT V., "Hypermédia et technologies Web", in *H2PTM'03*, Hermes-Lavoisier, 2003.

[QUI 08] QUINIO B., RÉVEILLON G., "Économie 3D et intégration des univers virtuels en entreprise : l'apport écologique des TIC", *Vie & sciences de l'entreprise*, vol. 2, nos. 179–180, pp. 76–93, 2008.

[RAB 95] RABARDEL P., *Les hommes et les technologies: approche cognitive des instruments contemporains*, Armand Colin, 1995.

[RAB 98] RABARDEL P., *Ergonomie: concepts et méthodes*, Octares, 1998.

[RAO 96] RAO R., "Quand l'information parle à nos yeux", *La recherche*, no. 285, 1996.

[RAS 00] RASTIER F., "Problématiques du sens et de la signification" in BARBIER J.-M., GALATANU O. (eds), *Signification, sens, formations*, PUF, Paris, 2000.

[RAY 94] RAYWARD W.B., "Visions of Xanadu: Paul Otlet (1868:1944) and Hypertext", *Journal of the Association for Information Science and Technology (JASIST)*, vol. 45, no. 4, pp. 235–250, 1994.

[RDF 99] RESOURCE DESCRIPTION FRAMEWORK (RDF) MODEL AND SYNTAX SPECIFICATION, W3C recommendation, available at: http://www.w3.org/TR/1999/REC-rdf-syntax-19990222/, 22 February 1999.

[REB 07] REBILLARD F., *Le Web 2.0 en perspective*, L'Harmattan, Paris, 2007.

[REN 01] RENSKY M., "Digital natives, digital immigrants", *On the Horizon*, NCB University Press, vol. 9, no. 5, 2001.

[REP 11] REPERE, *Ressources Electroniques Pour les Eudiants, la Recherche et l'Enseignement*, ENSSIB, 2011.

[RIC 96] RICHARD N., "Les autoroutes de l'information et le multimédia: vers quelle société?", *Terminal*, vols. 71–72, pp. 237–258, 1996.

[RIC 14] RICHTER F., Data journalist, available at: http://www.statista.com/chart/3570/app-usage-in-the-united-states/, 2014.

[RIE 06] RIEDER B., Métatechnologies et délégation: pour un design orienté-société dans l'ère du Web 2.0, PhD Thesis, University Paris VIII, 2006.

[RIF 05] RIFKINS J., *L'âge de l'accès: La nouvelle culture du capitalisme*, La Découverte, 2005.

[ROK 03] ROKEBY D., "Construire l'expérience: l'interface comme contenu", in POISSANT L. (ed.), *Esthétique des Arts Médiatiques – Interfaces et Sensorialité*, Presses de l'Université du Quebec, 2003.

[ROL 06] ROLAND M., "Bibliothèques numériques? Les réservoirs documentaires et leurs utilisateurs", *Congrès ABF*, 9 June 2006.

[ROL 09] ROLLA P., "User tags versus subject headings: can user-supplied data improve subject access to library collections?", *Library Resources & Technical Services*, vol. 53, no. 3, pp. 174–184, 2009.

[ROU 97] ROUET J.-F., "Le lecteur face à l'hypertexte", in CRINON J., GAUTELLER C., *Apprendre avec le multimedia, Où en est-on?*, Retz, 1997.

[ROU 04] ROUET J.-F., ROS C., JÉGOU G. *et al.*, "Chercher des informations dans les menus web: interaction entre tâche, type de menu et variables individuelles", *Le travail humain*, vol. 67, no. 4, pp. 377–395, 2004.

[ROW 92] ROWLEY E.J., *Organizing Knowledge*, Gower Publishing, 1992.

[ROY 03] ROY R., "Pour une approche conviviale de l'accès à distance aux collections des bibliothèques publiques", *4ème édition du congrès d'ISKO-France*, Grenoble, 3–4 July 2003.

[SAL 72] SALVAN P., *Esquisse de l'évolution des systèmes de classification*, ENSB, 1972.

[SAL 99] SALEH I., PAPY F., *Les bases de données pour l'Internet et l'Intranet*, Hermes, Paris, 1999.

[SAL 01] SALEH I., PAPY F., BOUHAÏ N., "HyWebMap: Structurer l'information sur le Web", *29th Annual Conference CAIS/ACSI*, Laval, Quebec, 2001.

[SAL 05] SALAÜN J.-M., *Bibliothèques numériques et Google-Print. Regards sur l'actualité*, La Documentation francaise, 2005.

[SAU 02] SAURET J., "Le cas des technologies de l'informatisation et de la communication (TIC)", *Revue française d'administration publique*, vol. 3, no. 103, pp. 445–449, 2002.

[SCA 94] SCAVETTA D., Les pratiques de production textuelle: du traitement de texte à l'hypertexte, PhD Thesis, University of Paris 8, 1994.

[SCH 00] SCHWARTZ C., "Digital libraries: an overview", *The Journal of Academic Librarianship*, vol. 26, no. 6, pp. 385–393, November 2000.

[SCO 01] SCOTT G., The road to Web services, available at: http://www.w3.org/2001/03/WSWS-popa/paper63, 2001.

[SEF 13] SEFCOVIC M., Interopérabilité? Quelle information pour quel public?, Conseil d'orientation de l'édition publique et de l'information administrative (COEPIA), available at: www.souvernement.ft,October 2013.

[SEM 03] SEMPRINI A., *La société de flux, formes du sens et identité dans les sociétés contemporaines*, L'Harmattan, Paris, 2003.

[SER 00] SERRES A., Aux sources d'internet: l'émergence d'Arpanet: exploration du processus d'émergence d'une infrastructure informationnelle: description des trajectoires des acteurs et actants, des filières et des réseaux constitutifs de la naissance d'Arpanet: problèmes critiques et épistémologiques posés par l'histoire des innovations, Thesis, University of Rennes 2, 2000.

[SER 05] SERRES A., "Évaluation de l'information sur Internet", *Bulletin des bibliothèques de France*, vol. 50, no. 6, pp. 38–44, 2005.

[SHI 06] SHIRI A., RUECKER S., ANVIK K. *et al.*, "Thesaurus-enhanced visual interfaces for multilingual information retrieval", *Proceedings of the American Society for Information Science and Technology*, vol. 43, no. 1, pp. 1–7, 2006.

[SIM 02] SIMONNOT B., "De la pertinence à l'utilité en recherche d'information: le cas du Web", in COUZINET V., RÉGIMBEAU G. (eds), *Recherches récentes en Sciences de l'information*, ADBS, Paris, 2002.

[SIM 08] SIMONOT B. (ed.), "Moteur de recherche. Usages et enjeux", *Questions de Comunication*, vol. 14, 2008.

[SIR 01] SIRINELLI P., "L'evolution juridique du droit d'auteur", *Réseaux*, vol. 6, no. 110, pp. 42–59, 2001.

[SMI 88] SMITH J.B., WEISS S.F., "Hypertext", *Communications of the ACM*, vol. 31, no. 7, pp. 816–819, 1988.

[SMI 03] SMITH M., BASS M., MCCLELLAN G. *et al.*, "Dspace; an open source dynamic digital repository", *D-Lib Magazine*, vol. 9, no. 1, 2003.

[SOE 05] SOERGEL D., "Thesauri and ontologies in digital libraries", *JCDL'05*, Denver, Colorado, 7–11 June 2005.

[SOU 01] SOUBRIÉ T., "Enseigner la lecture intime du texte littéraire grâce à l'édition hypertextuelle", *Document numérique*, vol. 5, nos. 12, pp. 181–208, 2001.

[SOU 03a] SOUTHWICK S.B., "Digital intermediation: an exploration of user and intermediary perspectives", *Proc. Am. Soc. Info. Sci. Tech.*, no. 40, pp. 40–51, 2003.

[SOU 03b] SOUCHIER E., JEANNERET Y., LE MAREC J., *Lire, écrire, récrire: objets, signes et pratiques des médias informatisés*, BPI, Paris, 2003.

[SOU 03c] SOUBRIÉ T., "AUKAPIWEB: Auxiliaire pour l'appropriation de l'information sur le Web. Du traitement automatique de l'information à sa manipulation", in POLITY Y., HENNERON G., PALERMITI R. (eds), *L'organisation des connaissances: approches conceptuelles*, L'Harmattan, 2003.

[STI 95] STIEGLER B., "Annotation, navigation, édition électronique: vers une géographie de la connaissance", in BRUILLARD E., BARRON G-L., DE LA PASSARDIÈRE B., *Hypermédias education et formation*, 1995.

[STO 01] STOCKINGER P., *Traitement et contrôle de l'information – procédures sémiotiques et textuelles*, Hermes Science, Paris, 2001.

[STO 12] STOCKINGER P., *Analyse des contenus audiovisuels: Métalangage et modèles de description*, Hermes-Lavoisier, Paris, 2012.

[TAR 07] TARDY C., JEANNERET Y., *L'écriture des médias informatisés*, Hermes-Lavoisier, Paris, 2007.

[TAS 14] TASSIUS D., Formation et pratiques documentaires numériques dans les bibliothèques universitaires en France, PhD Thesis, University of French West Indie and Guiana, 2014.

[TCH 11] TCHUENTE D., BAPTISTE-JESSEL N., CANUT M.-F., "Accès à l'information dans les réseaux socionumériques", *Hermes*, vol. 59, pp. 59–64, 2011.

[TGE 11] TGE-ADONIS, Le guides des bonnes pratiques numériques, version 2, available at: http://www.huma-num.fr/ressources/guides, 15 September 2011.

[THE 02] THÉPAUT Y., *Pouvoir, Information, Economie*, Economica, 2002.

[TIJ 03] TIJUS C.-A., CORDIER F., "Psychologie de la connaissance des objets. Catégories et propriétés, tâches et domaines d'investigation", *L'année psychologique*, vol. 103, no. 2, pp. 223–256, 2003.

[TIL 93] TILLEY S.R., WHITNEY M.J., MÜLLER H.A. et al., "Personalized information structures", *11th International Conference on Systems Documentation* (SIGDOC'93), Waterloo, Ontario, pp. 325–337, 5–8 October 1993.

[TOM 00] TOMS E., "Serendipitous information retrieval", *Proceedings of the 1st DELOS Network of Excellence, Workshop on Information Seeking*, Searching and Querying in Digital Libraries, Zurich, 2000.

[TOS 07] TOSELLO-BANCAL J.-E., "PERSEE: programme de valorisation des collections de revues francophones en sciences humaines et sociales mis en oeuvre par le ministère de l'Education nationale de l'enseignement supérieur et de la recherche", in PAPY F. (ed.), *Usages et Pratiques dans les bibliothèques numériques*, Hermes-Lavoisier, Paris, 2007.

[TRI 00] TRICOT A., TRICOT M., "Un cadre formel pour interpréter les liens entre utilisabilité et utilité des systèmes d'information (et généralisation à l'évaluation d'objets finalisés)", *Actes du Colloque Ergo-IHM 2000*, Biarritz, 3–6 October 2000.

[TRI 03] TRICOT A. *et al.*, "Utilité, utilisabilité et acceptabilité: interpréter les relations entre les trois dimensions de l'évaluation des EIAH", *Actes du colloque Environnements Informatiques pour l'Apprentissage Humain*, Strasbourg, 2003.

[TRI 06] TRICOT C., ROCHE C., FOVEAU C. *et al.*, "Cartographie sémantique de fonds numériques scientifiques et techniques", *Document numérique*, no. 9, pp. 13–35, 2006.

[TRO 05] TRONCY R., "Nouveaux outils et documents audiovisuels: les innovations du web sémantique", *Documentaliste-Sciences de l'Information*, vol. 42, no. 6, pp. 392–404, 2005.

[UNE 05] UNESCO (ed.), *Vers les sociétés du savoir*, UNESCO, 2005.

[VAN 88] VANOIRBEEK C., Une modélisation de documents pour le formatage, PhD Thesis, Ecole Polytechnique Fédérale de Lausanne, Switzerland, 1988.

[VID 12] VIDAL G. (ed.), *Sociologie des usages. Continuité et transformations*, Hermes-Lavoisier, Paris, September 2012.

[VID 13] VIDAL G. (ed.), "Instabilité et permanence des usages numériques", *Les cahiers du Numérique*, vol. 9, no. 2, p. 165, 2013.

[VIE 97] VIERA L., "Les processus de diffusion électronique: vers une désintermédiation des usages pour les publics universitaires", *Une nouvelle donne pour les revues scientifiques*, Villeurbanne, pp. 104–113, 1997.

[VIR 03] VIRBEL J., "La lecture assistée par ordinateur et la station de lecture de la Bibliothèque nationale de France", in VUILLEMIN A., *Les banques de données littéraires*, 1993.

[WAL 07] WALDNER J.-B., *Nano-informatique et intelligence ambiante: inventer l'ordinateur du XXI° siècle*, Hermes-Lavoisier, 2007.

[WES 09] WESTEEL I., "Le patrimoine passe au numérique", *Bulletin des Bibliothèques de France*, vol. 54, no. 1, pp. 28–35, 2009.

[WHI 13] WHITE H., "Examining scientific vocabulary: mapping controlled vocabularies with free text keywords", *Cataloging & Classification Quarterly*, vol. 51, no. 6, pp. 655–674, 2013.

[WIL 06] WILSON T.D., "On user studies and information needs", *Journal of Documentation*, vol. 62, no. 6, pp. 658–670, 2006.

[WLO 13] WLODARCZYK B., "Topic map as a method for the development of subject headings vocabulary: an introduction to the project of the national library of Poland", *Cataloging & Classification Quarterly*, vol. 51, no. 7, pp. 816–829, 2013.

[WOL 00] WOLTON D., *Internet et après?*, Flammarion, Paris, 2000.

[WOR 01] WORLD WIDE WEB CONSORTIUM, Workshop on Web services, available at: http://www.w3.org/2001/03/WSWS-popa/paper08, San Jose, CA, 11–12 April 2001.

[WOR 04] WORLD WIDE WEB CONSORTIUM, W3C publie les recommandations RDF et OWL, available at: http://www.w3.org/2004/01/sws-pressrelease.html.fr, 10 February 2004.

[YAZ 13] YAZDANI M., POPESCU-BELIS A., "Computing text semantic relatedness using the contents and links of a hypertext encyclopedia", *Artificial Intelligence*, no. 194, pp. 176–202, 2013.

[ZAC 10] ZACKLAD M., GIBOIN A., "Systèmes d'Organisation des Connaissances (SOC) hétérogènes pour les applications documentaires", *Document Numérique*, vol. 13, no. 2, 2010.

[ZOU 13] ZOUHRI T., L'implicite dans la requête adressée à un moteur de recherches, PhD Thesis, University of Lyon 1, 2013.

# Index

## D, E, F, G

## H, I, J, L

## M, N, O, P